G O D.

CONFERENCES

DELIVERED AT NOTRE DAME IN PARIS,

BY THE

REV. PÈRE LACORDAIRE,

OF THE ORDER OF FRIAR-PREACHERS.

Translated from the French, with the Author's permission, by a Tertiary of the same Order.

Catholic Authors Press
www.CatholicAuthors.com

Reprinted 2007 Catholic Authors Press

ISBN: 0978943295

Catholic Authors Press

www.CatholicAuthors.org

CONTENTS.

	PAGE
The Existence of God	1
The Inner Life of God	27
The Creation of the World by God	59
The General Plan of Creation	91
Man as an Intelligent Being	121
Man as a Moral Being	160
Man as a Social Being	200
The Double Work of Man	231

CONFERENCES.

THE EXISTENCE OF GOD.

My Lord,[1]—Gentlemen,

We have proved the divinity of Christian doctrine in a twofold manner; by its results, in showing that it produces that marvel the Church, to which nothing is comparable, and which evidently surpasses all human power; and also by showing that her founder is Jesus Christ, the envoy of God and the Son of God. The effects and source of this doctrine being divine, it is manifestly stamped with the seal of divinity, or, in other words, it is divine. It would seem then that our task is ended, and that having crowned the doctrine whose minister we are with the most sacred and certain of all characters, we have but two things to demand from you, or rather to impose upon you, namely, silence and adoration.

[1] Monseigneur Affre, Archbishop of Paris.

The Existence of God.

But the human mind is so formed, it has been so steeped in light, that even if it saw the very hand of God bearing doctrine to it, it would not be willing to receive that doctrine without receiving therewith the right and power to sound its depths. The road of authority is doubtless a just, a natural road, and necessary for our present state; but it does not suffice for us. For our present state includes the foretaste of the future promised to us, and in regard to that future, nothing will fully satisfy us but light seen by us in the very essence of God himself. We do not desire henceforth to behold that light in its infinite fulness; we understand that limits have been placed to our mental vision and to our horizon: but how feeble soever that vision may be, it is that of an intelligent being; how limited soever its horizon, it is an horizon traced by the hand of God. Our mind seeks light, and our horizon receives its rays. As soon then as a doctrine is proposed to us, from whatever hand it may come, we thirst to fathom it, to scrutinize it from within, to assure ourselves, in fine, that it possesses other marks of its truth than merely outward signs, however great they may be. I cannot escape from this law of our being, nor do I desire so to do. I respect it in you as in myself; I recognize therein our origin and our predestination. After having led

The Existence of God.

you then for so many years through the externals of Christianity, I must now, under the eye of God, pass the threshold of the temple, and, without fear as without presumption, contemplate doctrine itself, the daughter of God and the mother of your soul.

I do not promise to show you its absolute superiority; this can be done only by leaving the present world and reaching the bright shores of the infinite. But I promise you that in comparing it with all the doctrines that have endeavoured to explain the mysteries of the world, you shall easily discover in it an unquestionable and a divine superiority. I promise you that a light shall shine from it, which, without always attaining to evidence itself, will form at least a glorious dawn of evidence, and perhaps even at times a blending, as it were, of the reason of man with the reason of God. Your soul elevated by veiled truths, will see them gradually growing clearer in the dawn of contemplation; in that holy exercise it will become accustomed to flights before unknown to it, and at length wonder at the sublime simplicity of the greatest mysteries.

But where shall we find a basis in order to found doctrine and appropriate it to ourselves? Where shall we find terms of comparison and means of verification? We shall not need to seek far. God has placed near to us the instruments destined by his

Providence to lead us toward himself. He has given them to us in nature and in intelligence, in conscience and in society. This is the quadruple and unique palace which he has built for us; quadruple in the diversity of its constructions, unique in the relations which they hold to one another, and in our indivisible abode therein. As God is whole and ever present to every part of the universe, man is whole and always present to nature, to his intelligence, to his conscience, to society; he draws from them a life which constantly receives light from their reverberation, and which never leaves him in the solitary gloom of himself. Nature speaks to his intelligence, his intelligence responds to nature, both meet in his conscience, and society places the seal of experience to the revelations of all the three. Such is our life, and there all doctrine finds its verification. A doctrine contrary either to nature, intelligence, conscience, or society, is a false doctrine, because it destroys our life; a doctrine in harmony with these is a true doctrine, because it strengthens and enlarges our life, and because our life, taken in its totality, is heaven and earth, matter and spirit, time and space, man and mankind, whatever comes from God and bears with it a demonstration of him and of ourselves.

It behoves me then to show you the conformity of

The Existence of God.

Catholic doctrine with nature, intelligence, conscience, and society; and to draw from that comparison, unceasingly rising before you, rays of light which will lead us to the depths of the invisible and the immensity of the supernatural. This will form the last part of our conferences, and although it must necessarily employ several years, I cannot divest myself of a feeling of sadness in thinking that the day draws nearer when I must separate from you, and when I shall see no longer, save from a distance in the feebleness of remembrance, those great assemblies in which God was with us. Nevertheless some consolation is blended with the feeling of our coming separation; the consolation of the man who reaches his end, who has finished a career, and who foresees the hour when he will be able to say with St. Paul: *I have fought the good fight, I have finished my course.*[2] Share with me this sadness and this joy; for our conferences belong to you as much as to me; they form a monument which has risen up from your hearts and from mine as from a single principle; and some day, if it please God to grant us the repose of old age, we shall each alike be able to say, on recalling the times which we loved: I formed part of those conferences of Notre Dame which held our youth captive under the word of God.

[2] 2 Tim. iv. 7.

The Existence of God.

MY LORD:

The Church and the country thank you together for the example you have given to us in these days of great and memorable emotion.[3] You have called us into this cathedral on the morrow of a revolution in which all seemed to have been lost; we have responded to your call; we are here peaceably assembled under these antique vaults; we learn from them to fear nothing either for religion or for country; both will continue their career under the hand of God who protects them; both render thanks to you for having believed in this indissoluble alliance, and for having discerned in passing things those which remain firm and become strengthened even by the changeableness of events.

Doctrine is the science of destinies. We live, but why do we live? We live, but how do we live? We, and all that is passing around us, move by a motion which never ceases. The heavens move onwards, the earth is borne along, the waves follow each other on the old shores of the sea; the plant springs up, the tree waxes great, the dust drifts along, and the mind of man, yet more restless than all else in nature, knows no repose. Whence and why is this? All motion supposes a starting-point, a term to which it tends, and

[3] The Revolution of 1848.

The Existence of God.

a road by which it passes. What is then our starting-point? What our end? What our road? Doctrine must answer us; doctrine must show us our beginning, our end, our means; and, with them, the secret of our destinies. All science does not reach so far. The lower sciences teach us the law of particular movements; they tell us how bodies attract and repel each other; what orbit they describe in the undefined spaces of the universe; how they become decomposed and reconstituted, and numberless secrets of that restless and unremitting life which they lead in the fertile bosom of nature: but they do not make known to us the general law of motion, the first principle of things, their final end, their common means. This is the privilege of doctrine, a privilege as far above all the sciences as the universal is above the individual.

Now of these three terms which comprise the system of destinies, the one which doctrine should first reveal to us is doubtless the principle of things; for it is easy to conceive that upon the principle depends the end, that from the end and the principle proceeds the means. The principle of beings evidently includes the reason of the end assigned to them, as their principle and their end determine the means by which they are to attain and fulfil their vocation.

I ask then this supreme question, I ask it with you

and with all time. What is the principle of things? Catholic doctrine answers us in these three first words of its Creed: CREDO IN DEUM, PATREM OMNIPOTENTEM—*I believe in God, the Father Almighty.*

Hear its own explanation of this answer.

There is a primordial being: by that alone that it is primordial, it has no beginning, it is eternal, that is to say, infinite in duration; being infinite in duration, it is so also in its perfection; for, if anything were wanting to its perfection, it would not be total being, it would be limited in its existence; it would not exist of itself, it would not be primordial. There is then a being, infinite in duration and perfection. Now the state of perfection involves the personal state, that is to say, the state of a being possessing consciousness and intelligence of itself, rendering an account to itself of what it is, distinguishing from itself that which is not itself, removing from itself that which is against itself; in a word, of a being who thinks, who wills, who acts, who is free, who is sovereign. The primordial being is then *an infinite spirit in a state of personality.* Such is Catholic doctrine on the principle of things, the doctrine contained in that short phrase: CREDO IN DEUM—*I believe in God.*

Let us now hear the contrary doctrine, for there is a contrary doctrine; and you will never find Christianity announcing a dogma without at once meeting with a negation, a negation intended to combat it, but which must serve to prove it. For error is the counterproof of truth, as shadows are the counterproofs of light. Do not wonder then at so prompt an opposition to so manifest a dogma; invite it rather, and listen to the first expression of Rationalism against the first expression of Christianity: CREDO IN NATURAM, MATREM OMNIPOTENTEM—*I believe in nature, the mother almighty.*

You hear then that Rationalism, like Christianity, admits the existence of a principle of things; but for Rationalism, nature is the primordial, necessary, eternal, sovereign being. Now, nature is not unknown to us, and it is evident to us that nature is in the state of impersonality; that is to say, nature has no consciousness of what it is, it does not possess that intellectual unity by which each of its members should live of the universal life, and the universe of the life of the least blade of grass comprised in its immensity. We are, so to say, immersed in nature, we draw from nature the aliment of our existence; but so far from forming there one single life by common knowledge, we know nothing even of the beings nearest to us. We pass each other by as strangers, and the universe answers to our laborious investigations only by the mute spectacle of its inanimate splendour. Nature is deprived of personality, and this is why Rationalism, which declares that nature is self-existent, defines the principle of things as *an infinite force in the state of impersonality*.

Such are the two doctrines.

And observe that the human mind could not conceive a third doctrine upon the principle of things. For either nature exists of itself and suffices to itself, or we must seek its cause and support above itself, not in an analogous nature subject to the same infirmity, but in a superior being answering in its essence to the idea and function of a principle. It is the one or the other. If we choose nature, as nature wants personality, we must say that the principle of things is *an infinite force in the state of impersonality*. If we reject nature, we must say that the principle of things is a supernatural being, the logical conception of which necessarily leads to the conclusion that the principle of things is *an infinite spirit in the state of personality*. Therefore human reason, in regard to the first question concerning the mystery of destinies, the question of principle, is inevitably condemned to one or the other of these professions of faith : *I believe in God ;—I believe in nature.*

This is the reason why there are but two fundamental doctrines in the world : theism, and pantheism.

The first of these builds upon the idea of God, the second upon the fact of nature; one starts from the invisible and the infinite, the other from the visible and the indefinite. Whoever is not a theist is logically a pantheist, and whoever is not a pantheist is necessarily a theist. Every man chooses between these two doctrines, and the life of mankind cleaves to one or the other, as to the tree of life and the tree of death. Pantheism has perhaps been brought before you as a rare discovery of modern times, as a treasure slowly drawn forth from the fields of contemplation by the labour of sages : the fact is, it is as old as corrupted mankind, and the mind of a child is able to conceive that there is a God, or if there is not, that nature is itself its principle and its god.

It is a gift of truth, that upon a question so capital as that of the principle of things, you should have but to choose between two doctrines, and that on the rejection of one of these, the other becomes invested with the infallible character of logical necessity.

What do you now expect from me? You think perhaps that I am about to demonstrate to you the existence of God? I assure you I have no such intention, not because the thing is impossible, but because this is not the question before us. The existence of God is not a dogma overthrown, which it is needful to raise up again from the dust ; it is a dogma standing erect, which holds its place between the Church, whose divine authority I have shown you, and Jesus Christ, whose personal divinity I have proved to you. God has been the basis of all that we have yet seen. He has revealed himself to us as all beings reveal themselves, namely, by his action. If God had not acted upon earth, and if he did not still act here day by day, no one would believe in him, whatever demonstration metaphysics and eloquence might make of him. Mankind believes in God because it sees him act. We have not then to demonstrate God, but to examine the idea of God, and to place it before our minds in all the splendour that we can draw from it.

Let us even put aside those positive proofs of God ; let us forget his works in the world, and suppose that we have before us the bare question of his existence. The necessity of a direct demonstration of him would not even then follow. For our mind carries in itself the certainty that a principle of things exists, and, in addition, that this principle is either God or nature. Nothing remains then but to choose between them, and a matter of choice is quite another thing than a position in which reasoning has all to create. I have to oppose theism to pantheism, this is my task ; I have to seek which of these is in harmony with nature, intelligence, conscience, and society; such is the strength of my position.

Before entering upon this comparison, or rather on entering upon it, I will make one observation. It is that God is here below the most popular of all beings, whilst pantheism is a purely scientific system. In the open fields, resting upon his implement of toil, the labourer lifts up his eyes towards heaven, and he names God to his children by an impulse as simple as his own soul. The poor call upon him, the dying invoke his name, the wicked fear him, the good bless him, kings give him their crowns to wear, armies place him at the head of their battalions, victory renders thanksgivings to him, defeat seeks help from him, nations arm themselves with him against their tyrants; there is neither place, nor time, nor circumstance, nor sentiment, in which God does not appear and is not named. Even love itself, so sure of its own charm, so confident in its own immortality, dares not to ignore him, and comes before his altars to beg from him the confirmation of the promises to which it has so often sworn. Anger feels that it has not reached its last expression until it has cursed that adorable name; and even blasphemy is the homage of faith that reveals itself in its own forgetfulness. What shall I say of perjury? A man possesses a secret upon which his fortune or his honour depends: he alone upon earth knows it, he alone is his own judge. But truth has an eternal accomplice in God; it calls God to its help, it places the heart of man to struggle against an oath, and even he who may be capable of violating its majesty would not do so without an inward shudder, as before the most cowardly and the basest of actions. And yet what is there contained in those words of an oath? Only a name, indeed, but it is the name of God. It is the name which all nations have adored, to which they have built temples, consecrated priests, offered prayers; it is the highest name, the most holy, the most efficient, the most popular name which the lips of men have received the grace to utter.

Is it so with pantheism? Where shall we look for it? Come with me, let us knock at yonder door; it is illustrious, and more than one celebrity has already been there. We are in the presence of a sage. Let us beg of him to explain to us the mystery of our destinies, for he has sounded it. What says he to us? That there is in the world only one single substance. Why? Because substance is that which is in itself, and that which is in itself is necessarily unique, infinite, eternal, God. Behold then the whole

The Existence of God.

explanation of our life based upon a metaphysical definition. I do not now examine whether it be true or false, whether the conclusions drawn from it are legitimate, whether it is easy otherwise to define substance, and so to overthrow the whole structure of this doctrine. I simply defy mankind to understand it; even you, who from your childhood have been initiated to speculations of words and ideas, you would not seize its tissue without great difficulty were I to expose it to you. Many of you, perhaps, would not succeed so far; for nothing is more rare than metaphysical sagacity, than that vision which dispels before it all realities and penetrates with a fixed regard the world of abstractions. You would soon feel the swelling veins of your brow, a kind of dimness would seize even upon the most hidden recesses of your thoughts, and all would disappear before you, the real and the ideal, in painful obscurity. And we are to believe that truth lies hidden in such subtle and inaccessible depths! That there it awaits the human race to declare to it its destiny! Can you believe it? For my part, I do not believe it. I believe in the God of the poor and the simple-minded; I believe in the God who is known in the lowly cottage, whom infancy hears, whose name is dear to misfortune, who has found ways to reach to all, how humble soever they may be, and who has no enemies but the pride of knowledge and the corruption of the heart. I believe in this God. I believe in him because I am a man, and, in repeating with all nations and all ages the first article of the Church's Creed, I do but proclaim myself a man and take my rank in the natural community of souls.

Need I avow it?—Since I have been charged with the work of preaching the divine word, this is the first time that I have approached this question of the existence of God—if indeed it can be called a question! Hitherto I have disdained it as unnecessary. I have thought it needless to prove to a son the existence of his father, and that he who did not know him was unworthy of such knowledge. But the course of ideas constrains me to touch upon this subject. Nevertheless, in making this concession to logical order, I could not allow you to think that I purposed to satisfy a want of your hearts, or of the people and the age in which we live. God be thanked, we believe in him, and were I to doubt of your faith in him, you would rise and cast me out from amongst you; the doors of this cathedral would open before me of themselves, and the people would need but a look in order to confound me. That same people who in the intoxication of victory, after having overthrown many generations of kings, bore off in their submissive hands, and as the associate of their triumph, the image of the Son of God made man. (Applause.)

Gentlemen, let us not applaud the word of God; let us love it, believe in it, practise it; this is the only applause that mounts to heaven and is worthy of it.

I might here close this discourse since you happily show me that it is needless. Allow me, however, before doing so, to seek why the idea of God is popular, and whether that popularity is but a vain illusion of mankind.

We have said that we possess four means of verifying doctrines; namely: nature, intelligence, conscience, and society. If the idea of God be legitimate, it should derive strength from these four sources of light, whilst pantheism should necessarily find its condemnation in them.

Nature is a grand spectacle which easily exhausts our vision and our imagination; but does it bear the stamp of a being without cause, of a being existing of itself? Can nature say like God, through Moses: EGO SUM QUI SUM—*I am who am?* Infinity is the first mark of the being without cause; does nature bear this sign? Let us examine it. All that we see there is limited, all is form and movement, form determined, movement calculated; all falls under the straightened empire of measure, even the distances which remain unknown to our instruments, but are by no means unknown to our conceptions. We feel the limit even where our eye does not perceive it; it is enough for us to seize it at one point, to determine it everywhere. The infinite is indivisible, and were but one single atom of the universe submitted to our feeble hands, we should know that nature is finite, and that its immensity is but the splendid veil of its poverty.

If nature existed of itself, it would moreover possess the character of absolute liberty, or sovereignty: for, what can a being be said to depend upon which has no cause? But do we find this in the operations that manifest the life of nature to us? The universe is a serf; it revolves in a circle wherein nothing spontaneous appears; the stone remains where our hand places it, and the planet describes an orbit where we always find it. Those worlds, so prodigious by their mass and their motion, have never revealed to the observer anything but a silent and blind mechanism, a slavish force, a helpless powerlessness to deviate from their law. And man himself—man in whom alone upon earth appears that liberty whose traces we vainly seek for in all the rest—is he a sovereign? Is he born at his own time? Does he die when it pleases him? Can he free himself from that which limits and embitters his existence? Like nature, of which he forms a part, he has his greatness, but it is a greatness which so much the more betrays his infirmity. He is like those kings who followed their victor to the Capitol, and whose abasement was but increased by the remnants of their majesty. The spectacle of the universe then awakens two sentiments, namely, wonder and pity. And these, strengthened by one another, together lead us to see the emptiness of nature, and to seek its author. Such is the language of worlds, their eternal eloquence, the cry of their conscience, if we may give such a name to the force that constrains them to speak for a greater than they, and to repeat to all the echoes of time and space the hymn of the creature to the Creator: NON NOBIS, DOMINE, NON NOBIS, SED NOMINI TUO GLORIAM— *Not unto us, Lord, not unto us, but to thy name be the glory!* Yes, sacred worlds that roll above us, brilliant and joyous stars that pursue your course under the hand of the Most High, happy islands whose shores are traced out in the ocean of heaven, yes, you have never lied to man!

It matters little whether pantheism does or does not endeavour to pervert the meaning of the spectacle of nature. It is of importance for us to know, however, that man, taken in general, the man of mankind, sees at a glance that the universe does not exist of itself. Metaphysics will never destroy that deep impression made upon mankind by the spectacle of things which forms the scene upon which we live. A child perceives the incapacity of the heavens and the earth; he sees, he feels, he touches it; he will always return to it as to an invincible sentiment forming a part of his being. In vain will you tell him that he is God, it is enough for him to have had but a fever to know that you are laughing at him.

In contemplating nature, man sees realities; in contemplating his intelligence, he sees truths. Realities are finite like the nature that contains them; truths are infinite, eternal, absolute, that is to say, greater than the intelligence in which we find them. Nature shows us geometrical figures; the intelligence reveals to us the mathematical law itself, the general and abstract law of all bodies. It does more, it reveals to us the metaphysical law, that is to say, the law of all beings of what kind soever, the law which is as applicable to spirits as to bodies. At this height, and in this horizon, the universe disappears from our mental vision, or, at least, we no longer perceive it save as the reflection of a higher world, as the shadow of a boundless light; the real becomes absorbed in the true, which is its root, reality becomes measured by truth.

But where is truth? Where its dwelling-place, its seat, its living essence? Is it a pure abstraction of our mind? Is it nothing but the universe magnified by a dream? If it were so, our intelligence itself would be but a dream; truth, which appears to us as the principle of all things, would be only the exaggeration, and, as it were, the extravagance of sensible reality.

Shall we say that truth has its seat in our own mind? But our mind is limited, truth has no limits; our mind had a beginning, truth is eternal; our mind is susceptible of more or less, truth is absolute. To say that our mind is the seat of truth, is to say in obscure terms that our mind is truth itself, living truth: who is so mad as to believe this? Besides the contradiction existing between the nature of our mind and the nature of truth, do we not see the minds which form mankind engaged in a perpetual war of affirmations and negations? Truth would then be battling with itself? It would affirm and deny at the same time, although remaining absolute. It is the very height of folly!

If truth be not a vain name, it is in the universe only in the state of expression, and in our mind only in the state of apparition; it is in the universe as the artist is in his work, it is in our mind as the sun is in our eyes.

But beyond the universe and our mind, it subsists of itself, it is a real, an infinite, an eternal, an absolute essence, existing of itself, possessing consciousness and intelligence of itself; for how could it be that truth should not understand itself, since it is the source of all understanding? Now, so to speak of truth is to define God; God is the proper name of truth, as truth is the abstract name of God.

There is then a God, if truth exists. Would you say that there is no truth? It is for you to choose. I do not deny your liberty.

Perhaps you will still better understand the force of this conclusion by applying it to the order of conscience. Even as truth is the object and life of the mind, justice is the object and life of conscience. Conscience sees and approves a rule of the rights and duties between beings endowed with liberty. That rule is justice. But where is justice? Is it a simple result of human will? In that case justice would be but a convention, a fragile law called into life to-day and which may fall to-morrow. Is it an order founded on the very nature of man? But that nature is variable, corruptible, subject to passions that lead it astray. What is order for one would be disorder for another. If then justice be a reality, it must be an eternal and absolute law, regulating the relations of free volitions, as mathematics are an eternal and absolute law regulating the relations of material beings, and metaphysics an eternal and absolute law regulating the relations of intelligent beings with all beings, either existing or possible. Beyond this notion, justice is but a name which arms the strong against the weak, the prosperous against the needy. Now, this notion necessarily calls forth the notion of God, since an eternal and absolute law could only be a reality in the person of a being subsisting of himself, possessing a will active and just, able to promulgate an order, to maintain it, to reward obedience and punish rebellion.

Truth is the first name of God; justice is the second.

Now it is easy to conceive that there may be men for whom truth and justice are nothing but philosophical speculations, men who shut themselves up in the proud solitude of their own thoughts, and build up in them their own glory upon systems that bear their names. But it is not so with poor and suffering mankind: it needs truth for its nourishment, justice for its defence, and it knows that the real name of both is the name of God, and that the real strength of both is the power of God. The poor and the afflicted have never been deceived herein. When they are oppressed, they lift up their hands towards God, they write his name upon their banners, they pronounce to the oppressor that last and solemn expression of the soul that believes and hopes: I cite you before the tribunal of God!

The time of that tribunal comes sooner or later, its temporal and visible, as well as its eternal time. Kings even here below are cited before it, and nations also. It is the permanent tribunal set up in the midst of error and wickedness, and which saves the world. In vain would pride destroy it; the people saved by it save it in their turn. If there were none but sages among us, the idea of God might perish here, for a man alone is always powerful against God; but happily nations are feeble against him, because they cannot do without justice and truth. They protect him against the learned chimeras of false wisdom; they preserve his memory with a faithfulness which does not always preserve the perfect idea of him, but which at least has never yet permitted the sun and history to see a nation of atheists. Notwithstanding all that men have done, God remains as the corner-stone of human society; no legislator has dared to banish him, no age has ignored him, no language has effaced his name. Upon earth as in heaven, he is because he is.

But if God has on his side nature, intelligence, conscience, and society, what remains there to pantheism?

Where is it to find its basis? It seeks its basis in the obscurities of abstruse metaphysics; withdrawing from all realities, from every feeling and every want, in order to form a labyrinth from whence thought can find no exit. It loses itself the clue, and, shut up in the subtle prison which it has made, takes refuge in the sneer of self-deceived pride, and calling to its help, from the corrupted depths of ages, the prying spirits of subtle doctrines, it hurls against God and mankind the anathema of scorn. God passes by without hearing and mankind without answering. Let us do likewise, let us pass by also.

We have a threefold intuition of God: a negative intuition in nature; a direct intuition in the ideas of truth and justice; a practical intuition in human society. Nature, in manifesting characteristics to us incompatible with a being existing of itself, causes us to mount to its source; the ideas of truth and justice name God to us, without whom they would be nothing; human society, which cannot do without him, proves to us his existence by its need of him. But besides these continuous and inamissible revelations, there are others which divine providence scatters from time to time on the road of nations. He strikes with his thunders and rends the veils, he gives so full and deep a consciousness of his presence, that none can be deceived, and causes a whole nation to utter from its inmost heart that unanimous and involuntary cry: It is the hand of God! We are witnessing one of those times when God unveils himself; but yesterday he passed through our gates and the whole world beheld him. Shall I then remain silent before him? Shall I hold upon my trembling lips the prayer of a man who, once in his life, has seen his God before him?

O God, who has just dealt these terrible blows, O God, the judge of kings and arbiter of the world, look down in mercy upon this old Frank nation, the elder son of thy right hand and of thy Church. Remember its past services, thy first blessings; renew with it that ancient alliance which made it thy people; touch its heart which was so full of thee, and which now again, in the flush of a victory wherein it spared nothing royal, yielded to thee the empire which it yields to none other. O God, just and holy, by the cross of thy Son which their hands bore from the profaned palace of kings to the spotless palace of thy spouse, watch over us, protect us, enlighten us, prove once more to the world that a people that respects thee is a people saved!

THE INNER LIFE OF GOD.

My Lord,—Gentlemen,

God exists, but what does he? What is his action? What is his life? This question at once rises in our thoughts. As soon as the mind has recognised the existence of a being, it asks how that being lives; and still more so in regard to God, who, as the principle of beings, excites within us a thirst for knowledge of him, so much the more ardent and just as his action is the model of all action, and his life the pattern of all life. What then is the life of God? How does he employ his eternity? This is doubtless a bold question. Nevertheless it is a question which men ask and which they desire to solve. But how is it to be solved? How are we to penetrate the divine essence in order to catch a glimpse of the incomprehensible movement of an eternal, infinite, absolute, and immutable spirit?

Three doctrines come before us. One of these affirms that God is condemned by the sovereign majesty of his nature to isolation dreadful to imagine; that, alone in himself, he contemplates himself seeing only himself, and loves himself with a love which has no other object than himself; that in this contemplation and this love, eternally solitary, the nature and perfection of his life consist.

According to the second doctrine, the universe shows us the life of God, or rather it is itself the life of God. We behold in it his permanent action, the scene upon which his power is exercised, and in which all his attributes are reflected. God is not out of the universe any more than the universe is out of God. God is the principle, the universe is the consequence, but a necessary consequence, without which the principle would be inert, unfruitful, impossible to conceive.

Catholic doctrine condemns these two systems. It does not admit that God is a solitary being eternally employed in a sterile contemplation of himself; nor does it admit that the universe, although it is the work of God, is his proper and personal life. It soars above those feeble ideas, and, bearing us with the word of God beyond all the conceptions of the human mind, it teaches us that the divine life consists in the co-eternal union of three equal persons, in whom plurality destroys solitude, and unity division; whose thought corresponds, whose love is mutual, and who, in that marvellous communion, identical in substance, distinct in personality, form together an ineffable association of light and love. Such is the essence of God, and such is his life, both powerfully expressed in those words of the Apostle St. John: —TRES SUNT QUI TESTIMONIUM DARET IN CŒLO: PATER, VERBUM, ET SPIRITUS SANCTUS—*There are three who give testimony in heaven: the Father, the Word, and the Holy Ghost. And these three are one.*[1]

Here, and very soon after having promised you light, it would seem that I am leading you into a maze of darkness; for, can anything be conceived more formidable to the mind than the terms by which I have just expressed, according to the Scriptures and the Church, the relations that constitute the inner life of God? Do not, however, yield to this first impression; trust rather to my promises, since they are those of the Gospel, wherein it is written:—EGO SUM LUX MUNDI—*I am the light of the world.* And again:—QUI SEQUITUR ME NON AMBULAT IN TENEBRIS, SED HABEBIT LUMEN VITÆ—*He that followeth me walketh not in darkness, but shall have the light of life.*[2] Yes, be confi-

[1] 1 John v. 7. [2] St. John viii. 12.

dent, count upon God, who has proposed nothing to you unnecessary to be believed, and who has hidden marvellous treasures in the most obscure mysteries, as he has hidden the fires of the diamond in the depths of the earth. Follow me, let us pass the pillars of Hercules, and, leaving truth to fill our sails, let us fearlessly advance even to the transatlantic regions of light.

We would understand something of the divine life: the first question, therefore, we have to ask is: What is life? For, as long as we do not know what life is in itself, it is clear that we shall not be able to form any idea of the life of God. What, then, is life? In order to comprehend this, we must learn what being is; for life is evidently a certain state of being. We thus arrive at that first and supreme question: What is being? And we shall solve it by seeking for what is permanent and common in the infinitely varied beings which surround us. Now, in all of these, whatsoever their name, their form, their degree of perfection or inferiority, we find a mysterious force which is the principle of their substance and organization, and which we call activity. Every being, even the most inert in appearance, is active; it condenses, it resists foreign efforts, it attracts and incorporates to itself elements which obey it. A grain of sand is in con-

The Inner Life of God.

test and in harmony with the whole universe, and maintains itself by that force which is the very seat of its being, and without which it would become lost in the absolute incapacity of nothingness. Activity, being the permanent and common characteristic of all that is, it follows that being and activity are one and the same thing, and that we are warranted in making this definition: Being is activity. St. Thomas of Aquinas gave us an example when, having to define God, who is being in its total reality, he said: *God is a pure act.*

But activity supposes action, and action is life. Life is to being what action is to activity. To live, is to act. It is true that spontaneous, and, above all, free action, being perfect action, the birth or apparition of life is generally marked at the point where that kind of action is manifested. Thus we say that the stone is, that the plant grows, that the animal lives; but these different expressions mark only the gradations of activity, whose presence, how feeble soever it may be, everywhere constitutes the living being.

We know what life is. Let us advance another step, let us learn what are its general laws, and then apply them to God.

The first general law of life is: *The action of a being is equal to its activity*. In fact the action of a being can be limited only by a foreign force, or by its own will. Now a foreign force checks it only at the point where its own energy ceases, and as to its own will, should it possess any, that necessarily bears it as far as it can reach by its own nature. An action superior to its activity is impossible to it; an action inferior is insufficient; an action equal to its activity is the only action that places it in harmony with itself and with the rest of the universe. Therefore, whether you consider the general movement of worlds or the tendency of each being in particular, you will find them all acting according to the measure of their forces, and placing limits to their ambition only because they exist to their faculties. All, and man among the rest, advance as far as they can ; all, having reached the point which exhausts and stops them, write like the poet, proudly accusing their own powerlessness :

SISTIMUS HIC TANDEM NOBIS UBI DEFUIT ORBIS.

This first general law being recognised, I at once draw some conclusions from it touching the life of God; for as the action of a being is equal to its activity, and as God is infinite activity, it follows that in God there is infinite action, or, to speak still more clearly, that infinite action constitutes in God the very life of God. But what is an action? Nature and

The Inner Life of God. 33

mankind are composed only of a tissue of actions; we do nothing else from the moment of our birth to our death. Nevertheless, do you know clearly what an action is? Have you ever weighed the sense of that word which comprises all that passes in heaven and upon earth? An action is a movement; it is impossible for us to conceive its nature under a more clear and general form. The body moves when it acts, thought moves when it works, the heart moves when it conceives affections; from wheresoever the action comes, the tongue has but one term for expressing it, and the understanding but one idea for conceiving it. All is in movement in the universe because all therein is action, and all therein is action, because, from the atom to the planet, from the dust even to intelligence, all is activity. But movement supposes an object, an end to which the being aspires. I move, I run, I risk my life: Why? What do I seek? Apparently I seek something wanting to me and which I desire; for if nothing were wanting to me, my movement would have no cause, repose would be my natural state, immobility my happiness. Since I move, it is to act: to act is at the same time the motive and the end of movement, and consequently action is a productive movement.

Do not grow weary of following me; it is true I am

leading you by ways whose outlets perhaps you do not yet see; you are passengers in the ship of Columbus, you seek in vain the star that announces the port to you; but take courage, you will soon hail the shore, it is already near.

Action is a productive movement, as I have just shown, and, as action is the consequence of activity, it follows that production is the final end of activity; that is to say of being, since being and activity are one and the same thing. But in what proportion does being produce? Evidently in proportion to its activity; since, according to the first general law of life, the action of a being is equal to its activity. Therefore, to live is to act; to act is to produce; to produce is to draw forth from self something equal to itself. Doubtless we can conceive a production inferior to the being from whence it emanates; but that production, were it to take place, would not be the principal act of such life, it would but be accessory and accidental thereto. Every being tends to produce in the plenitude of its faculties, because it tends to live in the plenitude of its life, and it attains that natural term of its ambition only by drawing from itself something equal to itself. It is easy to prove this by observation, after having established it by reasoning. In what, for instance, consists the painful labour of the artist? The artist has had in his soul a vision of the Beautiful and the True; the horizon has opened before him, and in the luminous distance of the infinite he has seized an idea which has become his own, and which torments him day and night. What would he do, and what is it that troubles him? He would produce what he has seen or heard; he thirsts to make a piece of canvas, a stone, or words, express his thought as it is in himself, with the same clearness, the same force, the same poesy, the same tone. As long as he does not obtain that desired equality between his conception and his style, he is troubled and desponding, for he remains beneath himself, and sheds burning tears over the inefficacy of his genius, which is as a reproach and as death to him. *From him to whom much is given*, says the Gospel, *will much be required*. Such is the law of production, in the order of nature and art, as in the order of virtue.

But in order for life to produce something equal to itself, it must produce life; in order for the living being to produce something equal to itself, it must produce a being like itself, or, in other words, it must be fruitful. Fecundity is the extreme and complete term of production, which is itself the necessary term of activity. Thus we learn and lay down that second general law of life : *The activity of a being is resumed in its fecundity.*

Here the spectacle of the world around us is so striking, that it is almost needless to invoke it. Where in nature can we find any being so abject and disinherited as not to have received from God the grace to produce a being like itself, to see itself in another emanating from itself? The plant ceases not to sow in the earth the germ that multiplies it ; the tree sheds around it and confides to the winds of heaven the mysterious seeds that assure to it a numerous offspring ; the animal gathers its little ones to its unfailing breasts ; and last of all, man, spirit and matter, combines in his fragile life the double fecundity of the senses and thought. He bequeaths himself as a whole to a posterity which perpetuates him by the soul as much as by the body, a father twice blessed and doubly immortal. Shall I dare to advance further, and, passing from man to the opposite frontiers of life, show you the prodigy of fecundity even in those beings to whom science refuses organization, and which, notwithstanding their apparent insignificance, still find in themselves the power to seduce nature and be perpetuated in its bosom by alliances that manifest their vital energy ? In vain, from one pole to the other, from man to the worm of

The Inner Life of God. 37

the earth, I seek sterility. I find it only in one place and in one thing, in death. So that we may say with rigorous exactness, that life is fecundity, and that the fecundity is equal to the life.

Let us now lift up our eyes, for we can do so; let us turn them towards God. If what we have said be true, God, being infinite activity, is also, and even thereby, infinite fecundity. For, if he were active without being fruitful, if he were infinitely active without being infinitely fruitful, one of two things would follow, either his action would be unproductive, or he would produce only outside of himself, in the region of the temporary and the finite. To say that the action of God is unproductive, is to say that he acts without cause, and that his life is consumed in the powerlessness of eternal sterility; to say that his action is only productive outside of himself, is to say that his life is not his own, which is absurd, or that the universe is his life, which brings us to pantheism. We must then conclude that the life of God is exercised within himself by an infinite and a sovereign fecundity. Do not seek beforehand how this adorable mystery is accomplished; do not hurry your curiosity beyond the light and the abyss. Be masters of yourselves, examine the point you are investigating, hear the sounds that you hear, and no more. The infinite, in heaven, is seen at a glance; here upon earth it is difficult for us to lift even a little of the veil that hides it from us.

I ask you now but one thing, I ask you if you can form any idea of being without the idea of activity; any idea of activity without the idea of production; any idea of production without the idea of fecundity? I ask you if your mind consents to pronounce this judgment: God is infinite activity which ends in infinite sterility. You may say: He sees and loves himself, is this nothing? Yes, but his regard and his love are sterile; does that satisfy you? What! Your regard and your love are fruitful; they produce a living being like yourself, equal to you, in whom you see and love yourself; and God, the principle and pattern of all things, does not possess, under an infinite and a supernatural form, the mystery which you possess under a finite and natural form! His outer activity is great enough to give life to the universe, whilst his inner and personal activity is to produce nothing but the silence of unmeasured solitude! Is fecundity then a calamity, and sterility a state of perfection? If it be a state of perfection, do you not see that God contains them all in a supereminent degree? We must then conclude with St. Thomas of Aquinas, in his marvellous treatise on

The Inner Life of God.

the divine persons: *The consequence of all action being something which proceeds from that action, even as there is an outer procession that follows the outer action, there is also an inner procession that follows the inner action . . . and thus the Catholic faith establishes a procession in God.*[3]

Let us still advance and ask why fecundity is the sum or term of the activity of beings? Why beings tend to produce other beings like themselves, and, in fact, do produce them? The reason of this is contained in the very idea of activity and action. For an action is a movement; a movement supposes a starting-point, which is the acting being; a point to be attained, which is the desired being; and a relation between the principle and the end of movement, between the acting being and the desired being. Without that relation there would be no cause of movement, and consequently no more action, no more activity, no life, no being, nothing. Relation is the very essence of life, and we have but to examine our own life to find abundant proof of it. What do we from the first of our days even to the last? We hold relations with God, with nature, with men, with books, with the dead, and with the living. The very time that measures our age is a

[3] Question 27, art. 1.

relation, and our mind would lose itself in vainly endeavouring to imagine life otherwise than as an indivisible tissue of numberless relations.

What then is a relation? It is more than needful for us to know, since this is the last link of our whole being. A relation consists in the bringing together of two distinct terms. The perfect conjunction of these terms is unity, their perfect distinction is plurality, and consequently their perfect relation is unity in plurality. Survey the whole web of your relations, you will find nothing else there. The life of your intelligence is unity of mind in plurality of thoughts; the life of your body is unity of action in plurality of members; your life as a family is unity of affection and interests in plurality of persons; your life as citizens is unity of origin, duties, and rights, in plurality of families; your Catholic life is unity of faith and love in plurality of souls tending towards God; and so is it with all the rest. What am I now doing? Why are my words addressed to you? What is there between them and this auditory? Nothing, if it be not that my soul seeks yours to lead it to the seat of a light which, without destroying the distinction between your personality and mine, would, nevertheless, bring us together in the present unity of the same hope and in the future unity of the same beatitude.

Now this marvel of unity in plurality could be produced only by the likeness of beings, and the likeness of beings supposes their equality of nature by their community of origin. Fecundity, which produces beings like their authors and like each other, is then the natural principle of unity in plurality; that is to say, of the relations which form the life of beings by the continuous totality of their acts. It is true that we hold relations with beings to whom we are neither drawn by a similar origin nor by an exact likeness; but these relations are also feeble and distant, and the degree of likeness is always marked by the degree of kindred which measures the strength and intimacy of the relations. Thus members of the same family are nearer to each other than fellow-citizens; nations of the same race are more closely united than nations of different races; and all created beings derive from God, their common father, the reason of likenesses and relations, more or less direct, which bind them together in the vast unity of nature.

We are then entitled to lay down this third general law of life: *The end of fecundity is to produce relations between beings, that is to say, to give an object to and a reason for their activity.*

Already you cease to wonder at those prodigious words by which the Apostle St. John defined the divine life for us: *There are three who give testimony in heaven, the Father, the Word, and the Holy Ghost, and these three are one.*[4] You see that the mystery of life is a mystery of relations, that is to say, a mystery that involves these two terms—unity in plurality, plurality in unity. But before we arrive at a still more formal conclusion, let us halt for a moment to consider the effect of relations in beings.

Life is not the only phenomenon they offer to us. Above the movement that mingles and bears them onward, we find a charm which we call beauty. Beauty is the result of order; wheresoever order ceases, beauty vanishes. But what is order, if not the unity which shines in a multitude of beings, and which, notwithstanding their distinctions and their variety, brings them together again in the splendour of a single act?

Goodness is the sister of beauty. It is the gift which beings reciprocally make of their advantages, and consequently it is also the effect of relations. In order to give and to receive, it is necessary at least to be two.

Thus life, beauty, and goodness, have one and the

[4] 1 John v. 7.

The Inner Life of God.

same principle, which is unity in plurality; and to refuse this double character to God is at once to refuse life, beauty, and goodness to him. Would you do this? Even should you not understand how one and the same being could realize in himself one and many, unity and plurality, would that feebleness of your intelligence destroy the chain of the reasonings and observations which have initiated us into the most profound secrets of the nature of things? But let us meet the difficulty face to face.

God is one: his substance is indivisible because it is infinite; this is beyond doubt for faith as for reason. God cannot then be many by the division of his substance. But if he is not many by the division of his substance, how can he be many? How can a being who is one and indivisible at the same time be many? Gentlemen, I require but one word, and I ask you in return: Why should God need to be many? Is it not in order to possess relations in himself, those relations without which we can neither conceive activity, nor life, nor being? Let the substance of God, then, remain what it is and what it should be—the seat of unity; and let it produce in itself, without being divided, terms of relation, that is to say, terms which are the seat of plurality in relation to unity. For those two things, one and many, are alike necessary in order to form relations; and if the substance of God were divisible, unity being wanting thereto, relations would be wanting also.

I divine your thoughts. You would tell me that you do not even understand the expressions which I employ, and that there is manifest contradiction between the idea of an unique substance and the idea of several terms of relation to be contained therein without dividing it. I will show you that it is not so, and had you but the intelligence of a child, it would suffice to enable you to follow me and to render justice to truth.

I stretch forth my hand:—Where is it? In space! What is space? Philosophers have disputed about its nature: some have thought that it is an exceedingly delicate and subtle substance; others that it is something void, a simple possibility of receiving bodies. Whatever it may be, whether substance or not, space is manifestly a capacity constituted by three terms of relation, length, breadth, and height; three terms perfectly distinct, equal, inseparable save by an abstraction of the mind, and yet in their evident distinction forming together but one single and indivisible extent, which is space. I say that length, breadth, and height, are terms of relation, that is to say, terms which relate to each other, since the sense of length is determined by the sense of breadth, and so on. I say that these terms of relation are distinct from each other; for it is manifest that length is not breadth, and that breadth is not height. I say, in fine, that these three terms, notwithstanding their real distinction, form but one single and indivisible extent. This, moreover, is perfectly clear to the senses and to the mind. There is then neither obscurity nor contradiction in this proposition: God is an unique substance, containing in his indivisible essence terms of relation really distinct in themselves.

Shall I give a more positive example than that of space? For, notwithstanding the reality of space, you may perhaps accuse it of being a kind of abstraction. Take then the first body you meet with. Every body, whatever it may be, a stone or a diamond, is comprised under the three forms of length, breadth, and height. Prisoner of extent, it bears it in its simple and triple form, and becomes wholly incorporated in it by a reciprocal penetration which makes of both one single thing. Body is space, and space is body. Length, breadth, and height are body, inasmuch as it is long, inasmuch as it is wide, inasmuch as it is high. Divide the body as you will, change its inmost matter at pleasure, the same phenomenon of unity in plurality will always subsist; so that there is nothing in nature, space and body, that which contains and that which is contained, which does not fall under this definition as simple as it is marvellous—an unique substance in three terms of relation really distinct from each other.

The universe speaks then like St. John. Not only does it contain nothing contradictory to the logical rectitude of the expressions which represent the mystery of the divine life ; not only do these expressions take in it the character of a general and algebraic formula of beings ; but the force of analogy leads us also to apply this formula to the very principle of beings, to that being who should have placed in his works a copy only or a reflection of his own nature.

As soon, however, as we apply expressions or laws of the visible order to God, their proportions at once become changed, because they pass from the region of the finite to that of the infinite. You must not wonder then, if Catholic doctrine teaches you that terms of relation take, in God, the form of personality. Let us clearly understand this word. Every being, by that alone that it is itself and not another, possesses what we call individuality. As long as it subsists, it belongs to itself; it may increase or decrease, lose or gain ; it may communicate to others something of itself, but not itself. It is itself as long as it is ; none other is or will ever be so, save itself. Such is the nature and force of individuality. Suppose now that the individual being possesses consciousness and knowledge of its individuality, that it sees itself living and distinct from all that is not itself, it would be a person. Personality is no other thing than individuality having consciousness and knowledge of itself. Individuality is the characteristic of bodies: personality is the characteristic of spirits. Now God is an infinite spirit; all that which constitutes him, substance and terms of relation, is spirit. Consequently each term of the divine relations possesses consciousness and knowledge of itself, sees itself distinct from the others as term of relation, one with them as substance: its distinction marks its relative individuality; consciousness and knowledge of its individuality makes it a person. Imagine space become a spiritual being, you will have before you an analogous phenomenon. Length, breadth, and height would possess consciousness and knowledge of their relative individuality, consciousness and knowledge of their absolute unity in space; they would be one by substance, many by distinction raised to the state of personality.

It remains for us to consider how many persons there are in God, how and in what order they are manifested in him.

Up to this point we have only employed analogies drawn from external nature, but now, having to consider the number and genesis of the divine persons, we must seek in more distant regions a light approaching nearer to the light of God.

Our horizon and light are not limited to external nature. We come in contact therewith by our body; but it is out of us, even of our body, and in addition, it is but dust and ashes; and if we possess something of God, it is but a vestige and not an image of him. Let us leave the dust and limit, and enter into ourselves: Are we not spirits? Yes, I am a spirit! In this material sepulchre which I inhabit as a traveller, a light has been kindled, an immaterial and a pure light enlightening my life, which is my true life, which descends from eternity, and leads me thitherward as to my origin and nature. Why do I speak of time and space? Who shall stay me in these abject comparisons? Ah! I feel that you are ready to upbraid me. You wonder that I imprison my soul and your own in these inanities of the universe, where I see shadows only, and touch but the dead; from whence I have drawn only faint and defaced images of truth. You impatiently expect me to open to you the arena of a higher vision; I feel that it is there before us. I see that which is unseen, I hear that which is not heard, I read that which has neither form nor colour. Truth has still a veil, but it is its personality; it still has secrets, but they are the last. Nature, withdraw; and let us behold God in the spirit!

The mind lives, like God, of an immaterial life, and consequently it knows that life in which the senses have no part, and which is that of God. What, then, does the mind when, shut up within itself, imposing silence on all the rest, it lives of its own life? What does it, gentlemen? Two things only—two inexhaustible acts, which are constantly renewed, which never tire, and whose progress forms its whole labour and delight—it thinks and it loves. First it thinks, that is to say, it sees and combines objects divested of matter, form, extent, and horizon; a kind of universe before which the one that we inhabit by the senses is but a close and dreary dungeon. It dilates in that boundless sea of ideas. It calls into life, to form its own life, nameless and endless worlds which obey it with the quickness of lightning. It may be ignorant of their value and disdain them; pure contemplation will be so much the more burdensome to it as it exercises it the less and enchains its faculties to the abasements of the body. But I speak not of these treasons of the mind against itself; I speak of the mind as it is of its own nature, as it lives when it wills to live at the height where God has placed it. It thinks then, this is its first act.

But thought; is it the mind itself, or something distinct from it? It is not the mind itself, for thought comes and goes, whilst the mind always remains. I forget on the morrow the ideas of the eve; I call them up and dismiss them; sometimes they beset me in spite of myself; my thought and my mind are two. I speak to myself in the solitude of my understanding; I interrogate myself. I answer to myself, my inner life is but a continual and mysterious colloquy. And yet I am one. My thought, although distinct from my mind, is not separated therefrom; when it is present, my mind sees it in itself; when it is absent, it seeks it in itself. I am at the same time one and two. My intellectual life is a life of relation; I find again therein what I have seen in external nature, namely, unity and plurality—unity resulting from the very substance of the mind, plurality resulting from its action. What, indeed, would the action of the mind be if it were unfruitful? What would be its reason, its end, its object? The mind, like the whole of nature, but in a much higher manner, is then prolific. Whilst bodies divide in order to multiply, the mind, created in the likeness of God, remains inaccessible to all division. It engenders its thought without emitting

The Inner Life of God. 51

any of its incorruptible substance; multiplies it without losing anything of the perfection of unity.

You see that in rising from the outer to the inner life—from the life of the body to that of the mind—we find again the same law; but we find it, as was inevitable, with an increase of light and precision. Bodies, notwithstanding their marvellous revelations, kept us too far from God; the mind has borne us even to the sanctuary of his essence and his life. Let us enter, or at least, if we are forbidden to pass certain limits, let us approach as near as divine goodness will permit us.

God is a spirit; his first act is, then, to think. But his thought could not be like ours, multiple, unceasingly appearing but to vanish, and vanishing but to appear again. Ours is multiple, because since we are finite, we can but represent to ourselves one by one the objects susceptible of being known to us; it is liable to perish, since in the crowding on of our ideas one upon another, the second dethrones the first, and the third overthrows the second. On the contrary, in God, whose activity is infinite, the mind at once engenders a thought equal to itself, which fully represents it, and which needs no second expression, because the first has exhausted the abyss of things to know, that is to say, the abyss of the infinite. That unique and absolute thought, the first-born and the last of the mind of God, remains eternally in his presence as an exact representation of himself, or, to speak the language of the sacred books, as *his image, the brightness of his glory and the figure of his substance.*[5] It is his word, his utterance, his inner word, as our thought is also our utterance and our word; but differing from ours inasmuch as it is a perfect word which speaks all to God in a single expression, which speaks it always without repetition, and which St. John heard in heaven when he thus opened his sublime Gospel: *In the beginning was the Word, and the Word was with God, and the Word was God.*[6]

And even as in man the thought is distinct from the mind without being separated therefrom, so, in God, the thought is distinct without being separated from the divine mind which produces it. *The Word is consubstantial with the Father*, according to the expression of the council of Nice, which is but the forcible expression of truth. But here, as in the rest, there exists a great difference between God and man. In man the thought is distinct from the mind by an imperfect distinction, because it is finite; in God, the thought is distinct from the mind by a perfect distinction, because it is infinite: that is to say, that in man

[5] 2 Cor. iv. 4. Heb. i. 3. [6] John i. 1.

the thought does not attain to becoming a person, whilst in God it does attain thereto. The mystery of unity in plurality is not totally accomplished in our intelligence, and this is why we cannot live of ourselves alone. We seek from without the aliment of our life: we need a foreign support, a thought other than ours, and yet nearly allied to it. In God plurality is absolute as well as unity, and therefore his life passes entirely within himself, in the ineffable colloquy between a divine person and a divine person, between a father without generation and a son eternally engendered. God thinks, and he sees himself in his thought as in another so akin to him as to be but one with him in substance; he is father, since he has produced in his own likeness a term of relation really and personally distinct from him; he is one and two in all the force which the infinite gives to unity and duality; in contemplating his thought, in beholding his image, in hearing his word, he is able to utter in the ecstasy of the highest, the most real paternity: *Thou art my Son, to-day have I begotten thee.*[7] To-day! In this day which has neither past, nor present, nor future; in this day which is eternity, that is to say, the indivisible duration of unchanging being. To-day! For God thinks to-day; he engenders his

[7] Psalm ii. 7.

Son to-day, he sees him to-day, he hears him to-day, he lives to-day in that ineffable act which has neither beginning nor end.

But is this all the life of God? Is the generation of his Son his sole act, and does it consummate with its fecundity all his beatitude? No, gentlemen; for, in ourselves, the generation of thought is not the term where our life ends. When we have thought, a second act appears: we love. Thought is a movement which brings its object into ourselves; love is a movement which draws us out of ourselves towards that object in order to unite it to us and ourselves to it, and thus to accomplish in its fulness the mystery of relations, that is to say, the mystery of unity in plurality. Love is at the same time distinct from the mind, and distinct from the thought; distinct from the mind in which it is engendered and in which it dies; distinct from the thought by its very definition, since it is a movement of drawing together, whilst the thought is a simple perception. And yet it proceeds from the one and from the other, and forms but one with both. It proceeds from the mind, whose act it is, and from the thought, without which the mind would not see the object which it should love; and it remains one with the thought and the mind in the same fount of life where we again find all the three, always inseparable, and always distinct.

In God, it is the same. From the coeternal regard interchanged between the Father and the Son, springs a third term of relation, proceeding from the one and the other, really distinct from them, raised by the force of the infinite to personality, and which is the Holy Ghost, that is to say, the holy, the unfathomable and stainless movement of divine love. As the Son exhausts knowledge, the Holy Ghost exhausts love in God, and by him the cycle of divine fecundity and life closes. What more could be possible to God? As a perfect Spirit he thinks and he loves; he produces a thought equal to himself, and with his thought a love equal to both. What more could he desire or produce? And what more could you desire if, like him, you possessed unbounded thought and unbounded love in the unity of your substance? But, poor as we are, thought and love are in our souls only a perception and a possession of a foreign object; we are obliged to leave ourselves in order to seek our life, to appease our thirst for knowledge, our hunger for love. And instead of turning to the only source of truth and charity, which is God, we wed ourselves to nature, which is but a shadow; to the life of time, which is but death. Or, returning to ourselves in a hopeless effort, we ask from our own powerlessness the accomplishment of the one and triple mystery which is divine felicity; we endeavour to satisfy ourselves in the pride of a solitary thought, in the delight of personal love, and, like dust which consumes itself, we waste away in a withering grasp of egotism which would be infinite if nothingness could be infinite.

Oh! lift up your eyes to heaven! There is life because there is true fecundity. It is there that the spectacle of the laws of nature, and the study of the laws of your own minds, lead you. All teaches you that being and activity are one and the same thing, that activity is expressed by action, and that action is necessarily productive or fruitful; that the end of fecundity is to establish relations between similar beings; that relation is unity in plurality, from whence results life, beauty, and goodness. And that thus, God, the infinite being, the pre-eminently good, beautiful, and living being, is infallibly the most magnificent totality of relations, perfect unity and perfect plurality, the unity of substance in the plurality of persons; a primordial mind, a thought equal to the mind that engenders it, a love equal to the mind and the thought whence it proceeds; all the three, Father, Son, Holy Ghost, ancient as eternity, great as infinity, one in beatitude as in the substance from whence they derive their identical divinity. Behold God! Behold God, the cause and pattern of all beings! Nothing exists here below which is not a vestige or an image of him, according to the degree of its perfection. Space reveals him in its single and triple plenitude; bodies proclaim him in the three dimensions which constitute their solidity; the mind shows us a nearer vision of him in the production of the two highest things of this world, if indeed they are of this world, namely, thought and love; in fine, the very tissue of the universe which is everywhere but relations, is before us as it were a picture which the divine light passes over, penetrates, and so gives to us above the visible heaven a glimpse of the invisible heaven of the Trinity.

All laws take their source in this seat of primordial relations. If human society would aspire to perfection, it has no other model to study and to imitate. It will find there the first social constitution in the first community; equality of nature between the persons who compose it; order in their equality, since the Father is the principle of the Son, and the Holy Ghost proceeds from the Father and the Son; unity, the cause of plurality; thought, receiving from above its being and its light; love, terminating and crowning all the relations. These laws are full of beauty, and if legislators could realise them upon earth, they would produce a work whose privilege and secret have until now belonged to the Catholic Church alone.

Let us halt here. I have not demonstrated the mystery of the Holy Trinity to you, but I have placed it in perspective, where pride will not mistake it without insulting itself. Let us forgive that satisfaction to pride if it be jealous of claiming it. For yourselves, inspired by humbler and higher wisdom, give thanks to God, who, in revealing to us the mystery of his life, has not overwhelmed our intelligence by a sterile light, but has given to us the key of nature and of our own mind.

THE CREATION OF THE WORLD BY GOD.

My Lord,—Gentlemen,

We have penetrated even to the inner life of God; we know what he is, and what is his life. The course of ideas would lead us now to seek what is his character; but two words will suffice for us on this head. The character of God is perfection; whatever is included in the idea of perfection—immutability, wisdom, justice, goodness—must be attributed to God in an infinite degree, and forms his metaphysical and moral character. The difficulties which may spring from these divers attributes will naturally be solved when we come to treat of the relations between God and created beings. We pass over them then at a bound, and find ourselves logically in presence of this question: God being the admitted principle of things, how have they emanated from him? By what process, and above all from what motives?

The Creation of the World by God.

Here we begin to touch more directly the secret of our destinies; for they unquestionably take their source in the process by which we have sprung from the bosom of our cause, and yet much more in the motives that led the self-existing being to produce something which was not himself. What then is this process? What are these motives?

Before I answer, I beg your particular attention to the state of the question. We are not now inquiring whether the world is or is not a work: that question is judged. Whosoever is not a pantheist is compelled to admit that the world has a cause, that it is the work of a superior intelligence and power; now we have discarded pantheism, we have recognised God in the very infirmity of nature, and therefore we say of him with the people and the poet:

"*The Eternal is his name, the world is his work.*"

It is worthy of attention that the philosophers of antiquity who believed in the eternity of matter, such as Plato, could not however help recognizing in the totality of visible things the character of a studied work, and they called God the great architect of the universe. In fact the universe bears the visible sign of its personal powerlessness, if I may so speak; and those even who do not reach the idea of its creation, see in it the hand of the artist who formed and constructed it. They see it made, although they do not see it created, otherwise the idea of God would have no reason in their minds. The production of the world is a dogma which logically precedes the dogma of the existence of God. We say : The world is produced, therefore God is ; and not : God is, therefore the world is produced. It is the reasoning of the ancient theist philosophers as well as of the Christian philosophers, only it was less complete in the former than in the latter. Aristotle, for instance, after having admitted the eternity of matter, could no longer mount to a supreme cause, save by discovering something in nature whose presence could not be explained without a higher principle. Such to him was the movement of bodies. The analysis of this phenomenon led him to see the necessity of a first motor, and he wrote this proposition, which is almost divine in its depth and originality : There is something immovable which is the principle of movement.

Once more then we are not inquiring whether the world is produced, but how and why it has been produced.

Two systems have divided minds outside the pale of Catholic doctrine. The first affirms that the world

The Creation of the World by God.

has been produced by the co-operation of God and a certain inferior substance co-eternal with God. Picture to yourselves, on the one hand, the absolute and perfect being: on the other, a vile, shapeless, lifeless substance, unable of itself to rise from that abject state, and yet uncreated like God, eternal like God, self-existing like God—matter, in a word, and yet matter stripped of the glory in which we see it clothed; that had God left it there, it would be there still, a sort of empty and eternal tomb, receiving neither life nor death. But God beheld it, he was moved with pity at the infinite greatness of its poverty. He spake a word, and the world, bursting the inflexible bonds of its conception, appeared as our eyes now admire it, ancient in itself, new in form, father and son at the same time, son of one more perfect than itself, father of itself by co-operation.

This ingenious poesy has not satisfied all minds. Many have refused to accept it. Before logic as well as in itself they have seen the poverty of that singular substance, half God, half nothingness—God in the eternity of its being, nothingness in its powerlessness to give itself the mode of its existence—and in order to explain the birth of the world they have imagined the system of emanation. In this second order of ideas God has drawn the substance of the universe

The Creation of the World by God. 63

from his own substance, but without communicating to it his personality or his divinity.

Catholic doctrine rejects this system as well as the other. For either the divine substance is entire and indivisible in the world, in which case the world is God; or the divine substance is but in part in the world by virtue of emanation, and then it loses the absolute character without which the mind cannot conceive it.

It is not necessary to make a great effort of thought in order to seize the vice or rather the absurdity of these theories on the origin of the world. We find here a striking example of the strength and the weakness of the human mind. It has seen clearly that visible nature is inexplicable without the intervention of a higher nature; but—I know not why—it has not been able to determine the mode and measure of that intervention. Struck by the poverty of the universe, it denied to it self-existence in order to make it an emanation of the divinity; then, not conceiving either that God could come forth from himself, or that his substance became impoverished by that emission, it attributed to the world a fund of original vitality, but poor and held within the most extreme limits of incapacity. It is always the same contradiction. It would seem that only a little logical vigour was needed in order to draw positive conclusions in the fulness of truth; man was unequal to this. His eye, wandering between two abysses, dared neither to accept the one nor the other, and sought between them an imaginary resting-place.

Open now the Bible and read its first phrase : *In the beginning God created heaven and earth.* What simplicity, and what certainty ! Moses does not affirm even the existence of God; he names and defines him by an action which at the same time explains the universe. The universe is not eternal, nor is it an emanation of the divine substance; it was made in the full meaning of the word, it was made by a pure act of will. *God spake, and all was made,* said David, and this is the idea which the human mind was unable to discover, even in order to dispute it. The human mind ignored it, although it was the key of all, and, since it has been revealed, the human mind has rejected it as an incomprehensible fiction. What, says the mind, is it to make being by an act of the will? How can that magical operation be conceived? And what is an idea that offers no seizable image to the understanding? Man acts, but always upon a substance pre-existing his action; he produces, but only simple modifications in the subject where he exercises his power. Creation is an abyss in which he sees nothing

The Creation of the World by God. 65

but a name and despair; a name instead of an idea, despair instead of a solution.

What think you? Is it necessary for us to represent an act to ourselves in order to have an idea of it? Is it not enough that the force of logic constrains us to affirm its existence? I grant for the moment that reason in no way seizes the creating act; but it sees that the world is neither eternal, nor has it emanated from the substance of God, and, driven to the last extremity, concludes that it was made by means of creation; for what other issue remains to it? Assuredly if the mind sees anything here it sees but an impossibility, and therefore it takes the only road open to it, an obscure one however, but enlightened at least by the light contained in every logical necessity. Is it true moreover that the word creation represents nothing to our understanding? Is it true that we cannot conceive how the divine will is able to pronounce that sovereign word: FIAT! I should wonder if it were so; for, if we have unravelled in our intelligence images which have led us even to the sacred vestibule of the uncreated essence, why should not the mystery of our personal will teach us something touching the mystery of the divine will? The will is the seat of power; by it man commands and is obeyed. Command! What a word! Have you ever reflected upon it? One man

F

utters a word: it is heard, and all is in motion. Another speaks, nothing is done. Both pretended to command, one only has succeeded. It is because one only uttered the word that contains power, the word that expresses will. Many think they express it, because they speak the word; but few do so in reality. It is the most rare expression in the world, although it is the most often usurped; and when a man possesses its terrible secret, were he the poorest and the last of all, be sure that some day you will see him above you. Of such was Cæsar.

Have you ever remarked the part which the will plays in the occult sciences, and how no one becomes master of another there save by the energy of a kind of imperative fluid? Virile natures offer greater resistance to the perturbations of these secret arts, and this is why the ancient oracles chose the feeble mouth of the pythoness for their organ. Pardon this allusion to questionable mysteries; truth penetrates all, even those things whose nature is veiled and uncertain. Thus the clouds bear the sun in concealing it.

Be that as it may, none will dispute that the seat of power is in the will. It is by the will that man wields empire over his fellow-men, and by it also he moves his own body. Therefore, when Catholic doctrine

The Creation of the World by God. 67

teaches us that the world has sprung from an act of the divine will, it teaches us something which is verified by our own experience of the seat where lies the principle of our own force. In ourselves, as in God, the will produces force; but what is force? I stand still; suddenly my arm is raised, my hand is outstretched, my head is erect, my eye brightens: what has happened? Has any foreign power seized upon me and deprived me of my repose? No; within myself, in a calm and immaterial chamber, an act has been produced. I have said: Let my body move, and it has moved. At the same time I have conveyed to my members, and in an exact proportion, the quantity of force necessary to their movement; I have willed, and acted. Observe! the movement did not exist. It did not exist in my body, which was still: it did not exist in my soul, which is of a spiritual nature: I have produced it by a simple act of my will. I have created it. The proposition of Aristotle is verified in myself: *Immobility is the principle of movement.* What is this, but a creation? Say you that the motive power pre-existed in my will? Be it so; but what is the motive power but the principle that produces movement? Catholic doctrine does not teach that God creates without a creative power of which this will is the seat and the organ. The divine FIAT, like the human FIAT, has an efficient cause, without which it would be but an empty word, a fruitless desire.

Observe that the bodily movement is exterior to the soul which produces it by an act of the inner will. Herein lies the difference between generation and creation. When the mind conceives a thought, it engenders, because the thought is of the same nature as itself and dwells in itself; when the will suscitates the movement of the body, it creates, because the movement is not of the same nature as itself, and springs from without. These two acts have nothing in common. The first is the principle of the inner life ; the second of the outer life. The first is the life of God and of our soul ; the second is the life of the world and of our body. All activity is reduced to these two terms, to engender and to create, that is to say, to produce within and without. No being exists without this double faculty. Were the first wanting it would have no inner and personal life; were the second wanting it would have no outer life. Generation concentrates, creation dilates ; they form together the mystery of all life.

Judge now whether reason forms no idea of the creating act. It is true that in God that act assumes a strength which surpasses our feeble powers. Whilst the movement created by us decreases and soon dies, the things created by God strengthen into a durable substance. This is the same difference which we have already remarked between the production of the divine thought and the production of human thought; the characteristic of the work of God is subsistency, whilst whatsoever man does passes from being to nothingness with lamentable speed. But this passing away of our works does not destroy their reality, or their analogy with the works of the infinite. We really engender like God, we really create like him; we in an incomplete and a relative manner, God in a perfect and an absolute manner. And we understand the two mysteries of generation and creation, which form life, because we are really, although imperfectly, generators and creators.

This established, your place and your condition are henceforth known to you; you are not sovereigns, you are servants. Sovereignty is existence by itself; you do not possess it in any degree. You have been made, you have been *made out of nothing*, according to the energetic expression of the mother of the Maccabees, and at the very most you can but pretend to the title of children of God. This is the extreme term of your ambition. If the divine goodness has shed in your soul and upon your brow some traces of likeness to himself, you are his children, and he permits you, from your very dust, to address to his throne the name of father. This is your highest glory. Pretend not then to sovereignty; what is sovereignty in a being who lives by another? And yet there are men who would invest you with it. For this, rationalism strains all its efforts to prove the eternity of the world, and to seek for signs of indefectibility in ruin and death. For do you think that the human mind would rush so eagerly upon these questions if they did not involve consequences for the direction of the soul and life? Be sure that all is there. To say that the world is uncreated is to say that man is sovereign; to say that it is created is to say that man is a servant, or at most a son. The first doctrine gives us the right to define ourselves like God: *I am who am*.[1] The second places in our hearts the prayer of the Gospel: *Our Father who art in heaven.*

Between these we have to decide; we must live here below as God or as creature, in the modesty of obedience or in the pride of sovereignty. Which will you choose? Some sages will tell you that you are great; they take the sublime part of your being, and would persuade you that there is nothing above you. Others will place a low and dishonoured image of yourselves before you; in the lowest regions of your

[1] Exodus iii. 14.

nature they will discover secrets that will fill you with shame, and yet it is still but to flatter your pride. Catholic doctrine alone places you in your true position, without insult or adulation. It sees your greatness and proves it to you; it sees your wretchedness and shows it to you; it supports you against the pride that inflates and against the pride that dishonours you; in fine, it reveals to you at the same time the knowledge of your greatness and your wretchedness, in that single phrase which it alone has pronounced: Man is a creature, but he is the creature of God.

The creature of God! Why? What has moved that inaccessible being to look beneath himself and call forth that which was not? It concerns us to know, for it is evident that the beginning and end of our destinies lie in the motive of our creation. Lost as we were in the cold shadows of inexistence, unable of ourselves to rise from the depths of that tomb, we had no other hope, no other germ of life than in the will of God, and the will of God could only turn towards us, pity, and call us, by virtue of a motive which determined it. No reasonable being, in fact, acts without reason under pain of acting at hazard, and of ignoring what he does by ignoring why he does it. Therefore St. Thomas of Aquinas, seeking before us the motive of creation, begins by laying down this maxim : *Every being acts for an end;* and he calls the end by the name of *final cause*, in order to show that, being the motive of the acts of the will, it is really the principle of that which the will produces. God, in creating the world, was then moved by an end, that is to say, by an object which he purposed to attain, and which was the term of his thought, his will, and his action. What was that end ? If, in order to learn this, we study the springs of our own determinations, we shall easily find among them the motive of interest or of utility. We will and we act because we have wants ; our movements are the efforts of a being which does not live of itself, and which seeks from without the support or the increase of its life. But God has no wants ; he lives of himself, and in himself; nothing is wanting to the plenitude of his being and his felicity : how should he act from interest? How should he have created man and the world to fill the void of his nature, or to add to the infinite resources and delights not yet to be found therein ? Evidently he possessed them all, he had nothing to gain, nothing to lose, in the creation of the universe. The outward manifestation of his omnipotence was a supremely disinterested act.

It is true—I have often heard, and you have heard

it yourselves—that *God created the world for his glory.* But that expression has two meanings, one which is exact, and which I will soon explain to you ; the other, which is not admissible, because it supposes that the divine will may be moved by the reason of personal utility. Let us put aside, then, for an instant, terms ill-defined, and continue to seek what was the motive of God in calling the world into existence.

Man does not act from interest only : he is capable also of acting from duty, that is to say, of sacrificing his own to the common benefit, in the name of a supreme law regulating the relations between beings, and imposing acts upon them which turn to the benefit of others. This motive is infinitely more noble than the first : it draws the soul from egotism, and, as a moving principle, gives it an impulsion from above, which, being no other thing than the view and the sentiment of eternal justice, appears worthy to concentrate itself in God and to have commanded his resolution when he created the world. Nevertheless it is not so. God is justice itself. As soon as he acts, he acts under the empire of that law of equity which is comprised in his essence ; but before acting externally for the first time, before founding the universe, he owed nothing to it. He was free towards it in all the liberty which being possesses before nothingness. He could communicate existence to it or refuse it, according to his pleasure, without affecting any right, without neglecting any duty. Man himself owes nothing to nothingness, and in drawing forth another man from his generous bosom, he performs an act of full and absolute sovereignty. He is a father because he has so willed it, as God is a creator because he has so willed it.

But did no motive then inspire the creative will? It cannot be so, and this we have already shown. The motive exists; let us not grow weary of seeking for it in the mystery of our own deliberations.

Above duty, if it be possible, or at least in a place not less elevated and sacred, lies another moving principle of our actions: it is love. We advance, because we love; we suffer, we live, we die, because we love. Love guides our most ardent designs, and if we sometimes feel ourselves able to do all things, if, urging life and death before us with a force almost sacrilegious, we sometimes think that already we possess the energy of immortality, it is love assuredly, it is love that persuades us and bears us along. No courser is more rapid, none will ever bound over more abysses with greater pleasure, none will carry us farther, higher, or give us a stronger sensation of a being about to create. Was it then love that moved the divine will, and unceasingly urged him to create? Was it love who was our first father? But, alas! love itself has a cause in the beauty of its object, and what beauty could that dead and icy shadow which preceded the universe have possessed before God? That shadow to which we can give a name only by betraying truth! What could nothingness have said to the heart of God? How is it possible to love that which is not? Or even, how is it possible to love finite beauty when in possession of perfect and immeasurable beauty? Already love had produced in God its ineffable fruit; already the Father, Son, and Holy Ghost co-eternally respired in the intimate colloquy of their triple, and single, and infinite beauty. They saw, they felt, they spake together their beatitude, and all three immutable in one and the same rapture, they could neither see, nor feel, nor hear anything which merited from them a single sensation of their love. The mystery was fully accomplished—great God! and what remained then to move thy heart, and cause thee to see us from afar in that complete inanity in which we did not even wait for thee?

Something remained, do not doubt it, something more generous than interest, more elevated than duty, more powerful than love. Sound the depths of your own hearts, and if you find it difficult to understand me, if your own gifts are unknown to you, hear Bossuet, who speaks of you: "When God," said he, "made the heart of man, he first placed in it goodness." This is divine language, and had Bossuet uttered but this single phrase, I should call him a great man. Goodness! That is to say, that virtue which consults no interest, which does not wait for the command of duty, which needs not to be solicited by the attraction of the beautiful, but which leans so much the more towards an object as that object is poorer, more wretched, more abandoned, more worthy of pity! It is true, it is indeed true, man possesses that adorable faculty. I appeal to yourselves as witnesses. It is not genius, or glory, or love, that measures the elevation of his soul; it is goodness. It is goodness that gives to the human physiognomy its highest and most invincible charm; it is goodness that draws us together; it is goodness that brings blessings to misfortune, and that is everywhere, from earth to heaven, the great mediator. See the poor Cretin at the foot of the Alps: his eye has no lustre, he neither smiles nor weeps, he knows not even his own degradation, he seems as it were an effort of nature to insult herself in dishonouring her noblest production. Do not think that he has not found the way to some heart, and that his abjection has snatched from him

The Creation of the World by God. 77

the friendship of the universe. No, he is loved, he has a mother, he has brothers and sisters, he has a place by the cottage hearth, the best and most honoured place, because he is the most disinherited. The bosom that nourished him holds him still, and the superstition of love speaks of him only as a blessing sent from God. Such is man!

But can I say: Such is man, without saying also: Such is God? If God were not the primordial ocean of goodness, and if in forming our heart he had not infused into it something of his own, from whence should we have obtained it? Yes, God is good. Yes, goodness is the attribute which in him concentrates all the other attributes, and it is not without reason that antiquity graved upon the pediments of its temples that famous inscription in which goodness preceded greatness. But all perfection supposes an object to which it is applied. An object then as vast and profound as divine goodness itself was needful to it: God has found it. From the centre of his fulness he beheld that being without beauty, form, life, or name, that being without being which we call nothingness; he heard the cry of worlds that were not, the cry of immeasured misery calling to unbounded goodness. Eternity moved and said to time: Begin! Time and the universe obeyed the will of God, as the will of God had yielded, but freely, to the inspiration of goodness.

I say freely, because all the divine perfections operate within themselves in the mystery of the Holy Trinity, and because their outer action is thenceforth no longer necessary to their dilation, but a spontaneous effect of the free will of God. God was good before he created the world, and his absolute goodness was infinitely exercised in the eternal communication of the three uncreated persons. Therefore, when he made the universe, he made it from a free impulsion of his heart, and not from any necessity. He made it gratuitously, without the motive of interest, the constraint of duty, or the inducement of merited love, in the sole object of satisfying his goodness by communicating life. Therefore, St. Thomas of Aquinas, in treating this question, says that *God is the only perfectly liberal being, because he alone acts not for his own benefit, but because of his goodness.*[2]

This conclusion is of the highest importance for the whole course of Christian dogma, and it is needful to solve the difficulties which it presents, in the theological as well as in the rational points of view.

Theologically, a text of Scripture is opposed to us

[2] Summa, Quest. 44, art. 4.

which is thus written:—UNIVERSA PROPTER SEME-
TIPSUM OPERATUS EST DOMINUS—*The Lord hath
made all things for himself.*[3] These words possess a
character of precision and clearness which would seem
to overshadow all the ideas we have been placing
before you. It is however easy to explain them.
God could not, more than any other being, draw from
outside of himself the motives of his determinations.
He finds them in his nature, and in yielding to them,
if I may so speak, it is manifest that he acts for
himself, since he acts under the impulsion of something which is himself. But goodness possesses that
excellent and singular quality, that its object is the
good of others, and that in acting from goodness we
nevertheless act for others and in a disinterested
manner. Therefore it is true to say that in creating
the world from goodness, God has created it for
himself, since his goodness is himself; and yet it is
equally true to say that he created it freely, since he
intended the good of his creatures, and since that
good could not increase his own felicity. But even
had it increased his felicity, the motive of goodness
would still remain pure and irreproachable, for
nothing is more perfect than to find happiness in
communicating our own happiness. That egotism,

[3] Proverbs xvi. 4.

if such it be, is that of great souls, and although the creature may be profitless to God, doubtless we must believe that our love is not indifferent to him, and that, without increasing his happiness, it makes us dear and precious in his sight.

It would also be easy for me to explain that other expression to you : *God created the world for his glory*. The inner glory of God is in his sovereign perfection ; his outer glory consists in being known and loved by free intelligences; and it is beyond question that he has in fact given being to those intelligences in order to be known and loved by them. But why has he willed to call them to know and to love him ? Is it for their happiness or for his personal benefit? from the motive of goodness or that of interest? We have shown, with St. Thomas of Aquinas, that it was from the motive of goodness, and the expression under our notice decides nothing, since it does not even touch the question. It suffices to define the word glory in order to be convinced of this.

Let us now approach the objections of rationalism.

So far from admitting that the world is a work of divine goodness, rationalism does not even see in it a work of justice. Is it just, say they, to dispose of another's condition without his sanction ? When, in the exercise of his incomprehensible omnipotence, it pleased God to call intelligent beings into life; beings capable of judging whether existence was a blessing or a curse, had he the right to act without their consent? The Romans have written with as much eloquence as truth: NEMINI INVITO BENEFICIUM CONFERTUR—*There is no benefit without the will that accepts it.* By what right have we been made without our knowledge? By what right have we been drawn forth from nothingness to be thrown, without our consent, into that gulf of misery called life? What! we reposed peacefully in the eternity of our sleep, when suddenly an invisible hand seized upon us, a strange voice called us; it said with power: Come forth, see, feel, think, love! And, obeying that merciless order in spite of ourselves, after having spent hours or years amidst confused realities and vanished illusions, suddenly, again that hand which had dragged us from our first tomb, that hand rejects us! And the same voice which called us cries out to us: It is enough, lie down, close thy eyes, quit this world, begone! But if we were made for ourselves, should we not have been consulted in order to learn when, how, and under what conditions life was to be given to us? This has not been thought of: life came to us as death comes, with insult and scorn to us. Ah! let vain theology speak as it will, this is not the lamentation of the mind; it is the groaning of the soul, it is the sincerity of suffering and the accusation of the universe. Leave us, at least, to weep over ourselves, respect the desolation of ages, and do not add to the misery of our destiny that other misery of desiring to understand it.

I should be silent before the sound of those accents which have sometimes troubled you, and which perhaps still trouble many wounded hearts in this assembly. I should be silent, or rather I should lend my lips to the tremblings of complaint and ingratitude if I took in this question the same starting-point as yourselves. Yes, if this life were *the* life, if this light were *the* light, if this world were *the* world, yes, I should hide my forehead in my hands, and sink with you into an abyss of despair wherein I would hear no word of consolation. But do you believe this, and has Christianity so taught you? Do you believe that this life is *the* life, that this light is *the* light, that this world is *the* world? Do you believe it? and who has so taught you? I ask you again: who has so taught you? Yourselves, none but yourselves. Learn then this from me: I do not believe you. I believe that this life is a road, that this light is a shadow, that this world is a prelude. I believe that life is God, that light is God, that the world is God. And I believe with all my soul, at the price of my blood, if needful, that God has created us to live by him, to be enlightened by him, to find in him the substance of which all that we see is but an incapable and a painful image. This is my faith, it is this faith which I proclaim to you; and in order to dispute it you must deal with it such as it is, and not such as you make it in the injustice or discouragement of your own minds.

Yes, we all suffer: woe to him who denies it! But we suffer from the road and not from life. Life is abundance, peace, joy, fulness; when we love God we receive certain hallowed foretastes, certain yet imperfect delights, which suffice to make us forget the present world, or at least courageously to accept its passing trials. Is it meet, indeed, for a traveller awaited by unerring love, to complain of the road, to curse the dus he treads upon and the sun that lights up his way? For my part, born to sorrow like the rest, charged with the two wounds of my forefathers—anguish of soul and infirmity of body—I bless God who has made me and who waits for me. I ask not to be consulted by him about my condition; between the nothingness from whence he called me and the eternity he has promised me the choice is doubtful only to parricidal folly, and God should have counted upon my virtue as he counted upon his goodness. Eternal justice could not suppose the refusal of eternal beatitude : it was entitled to expect from us gratitude, love, and the acceptation of a trial without which love could not have been shown, and at least in ingratitude itself, silence and just remorse.

Nevertheless you continue, and you recall to me a thought which for a long time troubled the adolescence of my reason. If all of us, such as we are, intelligent and free creatures, attained the life of eternity, it is certain that the sufferings of the present life would vanish from our minds, not being *worthy*, as St. Paul says, *to be compared with the glory to come, that shall be revealed to us.*[4] But it is not so. Catholic doctrine teaches that a portion of created intelligent beings do not attain to the reign of God, and thus that creation, instead of turning to their happiness, turns finally to their eternal woe. By their own fault, it is true, but what does that signify ? God knew it, God had foreseen it. Was it an act of goodness to place beings in the world whom infallible foreknowledge beheld, whether or not from their own fault, excluded from the benefit of their primitive vocation, and hurled into a depth of ruin equal to the good prepared for them ? If God, in creation, had intended to act only in virtue of his sovereingty, by an act of power and choice, it might

[4] Rom. viii. 18.

perhaps be conceived that he had not looked to the result, and that the final misery of a part of his creatures, caused by their prevarication, might have appeared to him as an accident incapable of disarming the right and efficacy of his will. But you tell us that the supreme FIAT was pronounced from goodness, from the desire to communicate life and glory to possible beings whom God perceived in the horizon of his thought. Are this end and motive compatible with the eternal fall of the lost intelligences? Doubtless we admit that Catholic doctrine does not teach as an article of faith that it is the smaller number of mankind who are saved. Much less does it teach that in the totality of intelligent hierarchies it is the lesser number who maintain their titles before the justice of God. But what of this? Were there but one man, but one single intelligence disinherited from the true life and for ever reprobated, it would be enough to accuse divine goodness, or at least not to attribute to it the creation of the universe. Seek then another motive for the omnipotence of God; say that he has done what he willed to do because he willed it; that he was master, that crime and ingratitude could not deprive him of his sovereign rights. You may perhaps be listened to, but do not talk of the goodness of God in presence of that terrible image of eternal damna-

86 The Creation of the World by God.

tion: let us tremble before his justice, and be silent before his impenetrable majesty.

I shall not be silent, for what you have just said suffices to answer you. You admit that the creative power enters into the attributes which constitute the divine essence; it is impossible for God to be stripped of it by the disobedience of his creature. To say, in fact, that God has no right to create a being who might misuse his gifts, is to say that the wicked are able to destroy God by hindering the exercise of one of his essential attributes. What could be more vain or more unreasonable? Now, this admitted, the difficulty vanishes. In fact, even when God acts from goodness, he acts in the indivisible totality of his essence; he acts with his power, his wisdom, his justice, and all the inalienable totality of his perfections. Goodness moves him, but goodness which abdicates nothing of the rest of his divinity. Goodness could not hinder him from being wise, just, powerful, supreme, and if by his foreknowledge he perceive a creature so ungrateful as to turn his gifts against himself, he will not withdraw the blessing from him, since he would then take from himself the power to create under just conditions; this he should not do, this he could not do without ceasing to exist. You will say, perhaps: One thing is power in itself, another is the exercise of power; God could not lose power, but he is free not to exercise it. Assuredly; but you must understand that whosoever is free not to exercise a power, is free also to exercise it, under pain of not possessing it. If then you grant that God is free, all his attributes considered, to create a being who may abuse the blessing of life, why should you wonder that in fact he has exercised that liberty which belongs to him and which you attribute to him?

You still say, however this may be, metaphysically, the heart naturally rejects such a conclusion. Where is the father who would place a son in the world if he foresaw that life would even by his fault be a fatal gift to him? And is not God our father? Ought he not to feel more tenderness towards us than is felt by a mortal man?

Here the comparison wants force, because it is wanting in justice. God has not created isolated individuals, or even worlds; he has created one unique world in which all beings are linked together by relations of mutual dependence and service, and not one of these can be withdrawn without entailing the suffering of all the others. In the human race especially, each man contains a posterity in himself whose term is not assignable, and which makes of its generations one united assemblage in which no single member can lose his place without drawing after him the multitude of his descendants. To suppress a single man is to suppress a race; to suppress a wicked man is to suppress a people of just men who may spring from him. For good and evil are entwined together in the changeable course of mankind; a virtuous son succeeds to a bad father, and the ancestor but too often contemplates in his distant progeny crimes which to him were unknown. Now, the glance of God, perceiving at once all the successions of life, all the regenerations of good in evil and of evil in good, no destiny appeared solitary to him; so that in cutting it off from the anticipated book of life, he would but cut off a course unworthy to be continued. In his sight Adam, a prevaricator, included the whole posterity of the saints. To refuse being to him because of his crime, even had that crime never obtained pardon, would have been to destroy in him all the merits of the human race. How could the goodness of God have required such a sacrifice? How could it have required that the wicked should have been preferred to the just, that life should be withdrawn from those who would make good use of it, because of those who would have turned it into a curse instead of a blessing?

I know God, I love him, I hope in him, I bless him

The Creation of the World by God. 89

in life and death: why should the fault of one of my ancestors, eternally foreseen by divine goodness, have intercepted my birth, and not have permitted me for a single day to respire in the mystery of liberty from whence my beatitude might result? Why should I have been condemned to nothingness because one of my forefathers would have abused his existence? Where in this would have been justice, wisdom, or goodness?

God had not to choose between creating or not creating a wicked man, but between creating or not creating generations of good and evil together; and as all presented this mixture to his prophetic glance, he had to choose between creating the universe or not creating anything. The question is very different, and assuredly the most tender father would not choose to die without posterity, if God, revealing to him their future, were to show to him, in the transformations of his race, the inevitable alternatives of glory and shame, of happiness and misery. What would it be if, instead of a single generation, it were a question of all human generations? What would it be if to you were given the choice of destroying or creating the universe? For such is the question which was weighed in the counsels of God.

God has judged it, and heaven and earth proclaim how.

You may, however, judge it otherwise; you may complain of life and not consider it so great a gift. But learn that the life of which you complain is not that which God prepared for you, it is that which you have made for yourselves. You have cut off God from it, and you wonder that nothing remains. You have produced the void in your soul, and you wonder that the infinite is wanting to you. You have run after every vanity, and you wonder that nothing is left to you but doubts, darkness, bitterness, affliction. Ah! return, return to life, regain your rights in creation by the courage of faith, the holiness of hope, the divinity of love, and then, having returned to your place and your glory in the universal harmonies, you will repeat with all the worlds the testimony which God bore to himself after he had finished his work: *God saw all the things that he had made, and they were very good.*[5]

[5] Genesis i.

THE GENERAL PLAN OF CREATION.

My Lord,—Gentlemen,

In our last conference we sought to discover by what process or from what motive the world came forth from the hands of God; we have seen that it was by means of creation and from the motive of goodness. Goodness is, in fact, the characteristic under which the human race has always preferred to conceive God, as it is also that of the men who have, in the highest degree, attracted the love and veneration of ages. Whosoever has not been distinguished by this august sign has not reached the fulness of glory, and neither the fame of brilliant conceptions, nor the success of arms, nor scorn of life, have sufficed without goodness to uphold the remembrance even of Alexander or Marcus Aurelius. That of God, more especially, rests upon the same basis, and nothing is more natural to us than to repeat with David: *The Lord is sweet to all, and his tender mercies are over all his works.*[1]

God, then, having made the world from goodness, that is to say, in the design of communicating to it his properties, which are none other than perfection and beatitude, we must now learn the plan followed by him in the realization of that generous purpose. Now every plan is composed of two necessary elements; of the materials which serve to found it and the ordinance to be given thereto. I have, then, to-day to treat of the materials of creation and their general ordinance.

According to Catholic doctrine, God employed in his work, which is the universe, two perfectly dissimilar materials, namely, matter and spirit.

In the first place, what is matter? If I tell you that it is something possessing weight, you will oppose to me the imponderable fluids. If I say that it is something possessing extent, you will reply: Many philosophers consider that it may be reduced to atoms, that is to say, to points indivisible and consequently unextended. If I say that it is something possessing colour, you will object that it may easily be conceived as colourless. So is it also in regard to taste and sound. But this work of spoliation, by which we

[1] Psalm cxliv. 9.

The General Plan of Creation. 93

successively deprive matter of its apparent attributes, has nevertheless a limit where the critical effort of our minds must halt. Whatever we may do, there will always remain to it the permanent susceptibility of receiving form and movement. I say of receiving them, for we see clearly that it possesses neither thought, nor will, nor liberty, no personal activity or command. It is at the same time active and inert: active, since it is a force; inert, because it does not act spontaneously, but under the empire of an irresistible necessity.

Spirit, on the contrary, has neither form nor movement of translation from one place to another; it does not fall under the investigation of our senses. It thinks, it wills, it is free; no necessity acts upon it. In vain is it commanded, if it does not command of itself, and all the assaults of power are as nothing against a single soul that respects itself.

Such are the materials of the world. Catholic doctrine knows none other; the senses and reason reveal to us only these. Shall we here also find rationalism in our way? Yes, we shall find it; and again I remind you that Catholic doctrine will never establish a single dogma without finding that rationalism sets up a negation against it. It is so now and always. It is the nature of error to create resources against all truth, otherwise the liberty of our intelligence would be but a chimera.

If anything is clearly proved it is certainly the co-existence in the world of matter and spirit. What is more manifest? Matter is the object of our senses; they see, they handle, they feel it, they make use of it as they please, according to invariable laws discovered by science and verified by experience. No effort of the will is capable of destroying the impression produced in the whole human race by the constant spectacle of the universe. Spirit is not less evident and eloquent to us, it is even more so. For, spirit is ourselves. We have no need to place ourselves in communication with it as with an object foreign to us; it is intimately present to us; each of its acts reveals it to us in its special faculties, in its empire over matter and ideas, in its spontaneity and its liberty. Yet, who would believe it? two contradictory doctrines have appeared in the history of human reason; one which denies the existence of matter, another which denies the existence of spirit. Idealism maintains that all, in nature, is immaterial; materialism affirms that all is body.

And truly, if ever error could be a noble and a sacred thing, we should be entitled to say so of idealism, which pretends to deny the existence only of the inferior part of creation, and fails to understand what relations a substance deprived of all intelligence and sentiment can hold with God. Why, in fact, did Mallebranche, that illustrious Christian philosopher, say that, without the authority of faith, he should not believe in the existence of matter, if it were not because he could not explain to himself the object of God in creating it? And have we not ourselves shown that the object of God in creation was to communicate his perfection and beatitude to beings the issue of his omnipotent goodness? Now, in what manner does matter, incapable of knowing and loving, respond to that view of the Creator? How is it able to reach even the frontier of the divine order, where all is knowledge, love, comprehension? We can conceive the motive and work of God in creating spirits, images of his own nature, endowed with the privilege of scrutinising the invisible world, presumptive inhabitants of eternal glory, vessels of voluntary praise, humble yet possible companions of the most holy Trinity. But who will ever conceive the office of matter in relation to God, and even in relation to created spirits? If not eternal, why should it have been created for a day? If it is to outlive time, what will be its part in eternity, that is to say, in the pure reign of God?

Some ancient sages, endeavouring to penetrate this

mystery, had thought that the function of material substance was the limitation of spirits, which, from their nature, as they believed, had no barriers between them and the infinite. But sound theology rejects that interpretation. Created spirits have their measure in the divine will that produces them; since they are created they are limited, seeing that uncreated existence enters into the notion of the infinite. Let us suppose, however, that the immaterial and intelligent being meets with no limit in its personal essence, you cannot suppose that God would impose a limit upon it from jealousy—from fear lest it should become equal to himself—and therefore imprison it in the sepulchre of a body! Can you suppose that men are but gods enslaved to a sensible organization? Ah! had God been able to create infinite spirits, be sure he would have created them. He desired nothing more than to extend the orbit of creation; and you will soon learn that matter itself, so far from having become an instrument of restriction in his hands, has been one of the resources employed by his wisdom to enlarge the field of the universe.

Matter, like spirit, has been called to enjoy divine perfection and beatitude, and the more incapable it was of this the more God has willed to make nought of such difficulty, reserving to himself the glory, if I may so speak, of stamping the seal of his power and mercy upon a substance in which nothingness appeared to dispute the empire with him. However inert matter may be, however dumb, deaf, blind, insensible, it is indifferent thereto: listen to the Apostle St. Paul taking up its cause and speaking to you of its destiny: *All flesh*, he says, *is not the same flesh . . . there are bodies celestial and bodies terrestrial; but one is the glory of the celestial and another the terrestrial. . . . The body is sown in corruption, it shall rise in incorruption; it is sown in dishonour, it shall rise in glory; it is sown in weakness, it shall rise in power; it is sown a natural body, it shall rise a spiritual body.*[2] You hear that St. Paul is not troubled about the meanness of our dust; he does not believe in its final wretchedness; he beholds it so transfigured as to become spiritual, and if you would hear him again foretelling its future, listen once more: *For the expectation of the creature waiteth for the revelation of the sons of God. For the creature was made subject to vanity, not willingly, but by reason of him that made it subject, in hope: because the creature also itself shall be delivered from the servitude of corruption into the liberty of the glory of the children of God.*[3] What language! What splendour! What promises! Thus the most vile matter is in labour for its future greatness, as well as

[2] 1 Cor. xv. 39, 40, 42, 43, 44.   [3] Rom. viii. 19, 20, 21, 22.

man himself; it awaits the final revelation, which will distinguish the children of God and mark out a place for them in the ages which have neither shadow nor turning; it will take part in the deliverance of spirits, and their beatitude will, in a certain degree, depend upon its own, since its own will serve to the liberty of their glory. What singular expressions, gentlemen, and how truly may the substance honoured by such prophecies hold in contempt the premature insults of ignorance and error!

The king of Macedonia once said : " If I were not Alexander, I would be Diogenes !" Let me say : " If I were not spirit, I would be matter !" For I should still be the work of God, the fruit of his thought and of his goodness. His eye would still be upon me, and, united in human nature to an immortal soul, after having served it here below in its need I should one day serve it in its felicity, which I should share.

In proceeding to expose to you the general ordinance of the world, I shall, however, hope to show you the part which matter fills there, and consequently enable you more clearly to see the reason of its existence and its creation.

The other rationalist camp denies the reality of spirit. It aspires to convince us that there is nothing in the world but the palpable, divisible and miserable substance which falls under the investigation of our outer senses, and if it acknowledges the phenomena of thought and will, it attributes them to the very organism of the living body. You perceive that this doctrine is very different from the other. The first, although false, tended to the elevation of man; this tends to his abasement. The first induced us lowly to estimate the inferior part of our being; this tends to degrade, to immolate its superior part. What can have led sages—this is the name they bear—what can have led them to this parricidal act? The natural tendency of beings is to grow great; all, even those who obey only instinct, have a tendency towards pride. How is it that man, the visible masterpiece of creation, has employed his thought, which raises him above all the others, to destroy the very basis of his greatness, and to descend by his own choice from the rank of immortal intelligences? I know not whether there are any materialists in this assembly, and you know with what pious respect I am accustomed to treat, not error, but individuals. On this occasion, however, I cannot curb the liberty of my ministration, and I shall fearlessly say that materialism is a doctrine against nature, an abject doctrine, whose origin can only be explained by the corruption of the human heart. We are too manifestly spirits, there are not reasons enough against the dignity of our being to lead us to depreciate our own selves, if passions of a lower and dastardly order did not rise up within us against ourselves, in order to dethrone, with our spiritual essence, our ideas of truth, justice, order, responsibility—illustrious and incorruptible guests whose presence wearies vice and excites revolt. Vice knows no peace and wills to possess it. The soul opposes to it remorse, that last crown of corrupted man, that domestic and sacred voice which invites us to good, that good genius of the republic which inhabits ruins, and which appeared again to Brutus, in the fields of Pharsala, on the eve of the day when Rome was to fall. Oh !—pardon my doubts !—But if you were not pure, if remorse troubled you with its stern voice, in mercy and love for yourselves, do not drive it from you : as long as it is the companion of your soul you will not have lost the remains of your greatness and your hope ; remorse precedes virtue as the dawn precedes the day, and vice should respect it out of respect for itself.

But when vice has no longer the instinct of its rehabilitation, remorse becomes its chief and last enemy, and spares nothing in order to extirpate its very roots, which is our mind itself. Materialism is the result of that exterminating war of evil against good; it is no other thing than the supreme effort to stifle remorse. And this is why I call it an abject and an unnatural doctrine. If this should seem rash, I offer no excuse for it. What! You attack my very essence, you reject me to the limits of mere animality, you treat me as the equal of a dog! What do I say?—you dare to write that "Man is a digestive tube pierced at both ends." . . . Ah! gentlemen, do not laugh; it would grieve me bitterly to have excited your laughter; hear, hear these things with the silence of scorn. What! men dare to write that "man is a digestive tube pierced at both ends," and, armed in all the greatness of truth against imposture, shall I not turn back in scorn and trample under foot that most vile doctrine?

I ought to say no more on this subject; I ought not to give so much honour to materialism as to ask it to explain itself. We will do so, however, with your permission. We will ask these proud gladiators of matter what they have seen in man to lead them to contest his intelligent and free nature. Do they deny the phenomena of thought? Are they blind to those of the will? No, they admit them; they admit that something extraordinary takes place within us which resembles nothing that falls under the investigation of the senses. But they consider that earth, having attained to a certain degree of perfection, is susceptible of producing sentiment, thought, and will, as it produces roots, flowers, and fruit. Nature, they say, is in a progressive labour which is nowhere interrupted, and which at each degree is manifested by a more perfect production. Man is the term of that fertile progression; he unites in himself all the anterior progressions, and his brain, the masterpiece of the wisest organization, causes thought to emerge from it as naturally as the tree puts forth its buds.

How is it that this ingenious picture, for I will not call it analysis, has excited only coldness and incredulity in nearly the whole of mankind? How is it that the spiritualist philosophy has always obtained the glory of moving the heart of the people as well as that of the thinker; whilst materialism, a doctrine of decadency, seduces only a few souls in declining nations? Because spirit affirms itself with a presence so vigorous that reasoning and analysis perish before the splendour of that affirmation. How should it be otherwise? My spiritual being is myself: I feel the truth of it. I feel the distinction between my soul and my body with such force that my whole life appears to me to be but a confronting of the one with the other, and that each instant brings to me a conviction of their duality as strong as the certainty of their union. I see that I am two and one with a clearness which nothing diminishes, because nothing combats against the real presence of things. And what indeed is said against it? They oppose to it a progression of matter; but a progression is but the development of a germ which never changes its nature in that development. Elevate a force, according to the mathematical expression, to the second, the third, the tenth power; you will never gather in the force doubled, tripled, decupled, anything but the primitive element contained therein. In order that matter, transfigured in its form, may produce sentiment, thought, and will, the smallest material particle must be a being exercising feeling, thought, and volition, but in an inferior degree, susceptible of increase or of perfection as it is seen in the infancy of man compared with his maturity. Now, is it so? Does materialism even pretend that it is so? It does not believe that a grain of dust includes in miniature the intellectual functions of man, as a drop of water includes the properties of the ocean. Common sense too strongly rejects such folly, consequently matter elevated by organization to whatever point you will, to the hundredth or the thousandth power, will never produce anything but the development of what it is, that is to say, more perfect forms, more complicated movements, sculpture and architecture more worthy of admiration.

Men wonder—and it is another objection against spiritualism—at the reciprocal influence which the soul and the body exercise over each other. Why not, if they are really united? This union may appear strange, inexplicable, but what of that? It is a fact. The fact once proved by the certainty which we have of our double nature, spiritual and material in one sole personality, it is very natural that there should be an action of one upon the other, without which there would be no communication between them; and if there were no communication between them, they would be separated instead of being united.

Thus even as exterior objects, acting upon the brain by the intermediary of the senses, convey to the soul impressions from without, the soul in its turn conveys to the brain, and by it to the rest of the sensible organization, the rebound of its intimate and immaterial life. Thence arise those inveterate habits which take their source at the same time in the two parts of our being, both being in some manner bent thereto by the repetition of the acts, and become the slaves of our depraved wills after having been at first only their instruments. It is this which has given birth to that new science of phrenology, which abuses phenomena of the correspondence of the soul with the body and the body with the soul, in order to attack the free-will of man. I do not examine whether aptitudes and passions have really a representative sign in the exterior envelope of the brain; let us suppose it. What does it prove against human liberty? It is manifest that the soul and the body are in unceasing communication, and that every act—even an inward act—of vice or virtue, resounds somewhere in our mortal envelope and marks out traces of happiness or misery. These subtle traces, in their turn, react upon the profound seat of our internal activity, and solicit there the return of the same movements, that is to say, of the same thoughts and the same desires. Catholic doctrine consents to this; it does more than consent: it is the basis of its spiritual therapeutics, or, if you prefer it, of the medicinal treatment which it applies to the maladies of our soul. This is why the Gospel commands Christians to chastise their bodies in order to liberate and purify their hearts. This is why the Church imposes abstinences and fasts; this is why she commands labour, and why, after the example of Jesus Christ, her founder, she blesses those who weep and suffer; because, besides the benefit of an accepted expiation, there is in the afflictions of the body the infallible efficacy of reforming the senses. However ancient, however powerful, may be the traces of sin in the mysterious recesses of the body, the soul, aided by grace, fortified by penance, is able slowly to efface them, and to substitute the restoring vestiges of virtue. Thence, even in physiognomy, spring those singular illuminations which penetrate through the obscure traces of vice. The soul, after having ennobled the subterranean regions which crime had polluted, reaches the brow of man, and sheds upon it those serene and holy rays which soften the regard even of those who know not God. The gloomy shadows of sin fly away before the creative glory of virtue, and that which still remains of them in the premature sinking of the body is only a sign of mortality vanquished by the eternal beauty of Christ.

O visages of the saints! gentle yet firm lips accustomed to name the name of God and kiss the cross of his Son; regards full of kindness and love which perceived a brother in the most poor and lowly among creatures; hair silvered by meditation on eternity, sacred rays of the soul resplendent in old age and in death: happy are those who have beheld them! more happy those who have understood them and received from their transfigured glebe lessons of wisdom and immortality!

But what am I doing?—Am I pretending to demonstrate to you the existence of spirit, the reality of matter? God forbid! I do not stand before you as a philosopher, supported by his reason alone, and trusting only to the discoveries of his own sagacity. I stand here as the envoy of God, as one who bears his word to you, as one armed with the tradition and authority of the Church, and after having established the titles of my mission, I promised you only that rationalism should never oppose to a single Christian dogma negations more probable than the affirmations of faith. Once more I have kept my promise. For I ask, between the faith that affirms the presence in the world of two constitutive elements, matter and spirit, and the rationalism that denies the one or the other, where, even humanly speaking, lies the greater probability of truth? I do not say the certainty, because having found certainty in the order of the divine teachings, it is unnecessary for me again to seek it even there, where, in so many ways, I should be sure to find it. Against rationalism the semblance of truth will suffice for me, and I believe I possess it, and much more, in that question of the double nature of things. Let us hasten now to see the ordinance which God has given them; we shall gather here some rays of light upon the motives that induced the Creator not to content himself, in the structure of the world, with only one order of materials.

We have said that God, in drawing beings forth from nothingness, proposed to communicate to them his perfection and beatitude. Now the divine perfection is of three kinds; it is metaphysical, intellectual, and moral, and consequently it should be reflected under this triple aspect in the production and disposition of the universe. Let us commence by the metaphysical aspect, which is naturally the first.

God is infinite, he is one, he is many; it is the reunion of these three terms that constitutes his metaphysical perfection. He is great in the depths of his essence, by infinity, unity, and plurality; and this also should be the fount of the grandeur of the universe. But even thereby, the creating thought appears at the very first to meet with an insurmountable obstacle; for, the infinite is incommunicable in its nature. As soon as a thing is created, however vast it may be, it does not exist of itself, and therefore the radical attribute of the infinite is wanting to it. Nevertheless, the world—the work of the infinite in person, the manifestation of his glory—could not be wanting in extent, representative of uncreated immensity. It needed a projection which manifested its origin, and by which every eye on beholding it revolving in the

The General Plan of Creation.

majesty of its orbit might recognise the hand that had launched it forth upon a course and in a space worthy of it. God provided for this. He devised—if I may be permitted to animate the divine action by these human expressions—he devised, between the infinite and the finite, something intermediary, which here below we call the indefinite. I will explain these terms if you will allow me. The infinite is that which has neither beginning nor end; the finite is that which has a beginning and an end; the indefinite is that which expands between two terms infinitely distant, in such a manner as continually to draw nearer to them. God then resolved to construct the world upon the projection of the indefinite, and thus to impart to his work a figurative character of his unlimited essence.

Nothing opposed this design. Between God, who was about to create, and the nothingness whence being was about to emerge; between God, who is all, and nothingness, which is nothing, there existed of itself an infinite distance. It sufficed to fill it by a progressive creation, which, starting from an unique centre, should tend at the same time, and upon two different roads, towards the two extremities of things; towards nothingness by a graduated diminution, towards God by a constant ascension. But this plan supposed the existence of two quite dissimilar elements; one susceptible of constant diminution in descending towards the negative pole of creation, another capable of constantly perfecting itself in mounting towards the positive or divine pole. You anticipate me, you name matter and spirit: spirit, which is indivisible; matter, unceasingly divided: spirit, the element of the infinitely great; matter, the spirit of the infinitely little: both, in their diverse natures, sufficient to fill by their calculated elevation and degradation the infinite space which separates the supremely imperfect from the supremely perfect. It is St. Augustine who has revealed to us in a single phrase this beautiful law of the Genesis of things: listen to this great man: DUO FECISTI, DOMINE, UNUM PROPÉ NIHIL, SCILICET MATERIAM PRIMAM; ALTERUM PROPÉ TE, SCILICET ANGELUM—*Thou hast made two things, O God; one near to nothingness, which is primary matter; the other near to thyself, which is pure spirit.* In virtue of that conception, which was as it were the exordium of the world, God created two lines or two series of beings; one series descending on the side of nothingness, the other ascending towards himself. The one is known to you by your own senses and by the instruments with which science has endowed the eye of man; the other is revealed to us by faith, and also by the inductions of analogy. For how could we believe that creation stops at ourselves, and that having by our bodies an inferior kindred which extends even into the regions of the imperceptible, we should not have by our spiritual essence a superior kindred which penetrates even into the region of the substantial infinite? Faith teaches us this, reason confirms it to us, the order of the universe absolutely requires it.

Launched from earth to heaven upon that infinite projection, the world, as far as it was possible, had a relation of greatness with God; and by the innumerable multiplication of beings appertaining to each series, and to each degree of these series, it possessed also the divine character of plurality. But unity, the third term of the metaphysical perfection of God, was still wanting to it. There were two worlds, the world of matter and the world of spirit; the terrestrial and the celestial worlds: a supreme unfitness which deprived creation of all harmony and all possibility of being the mirror of its author. But how was this to be remedied? How were two orders so distinct, so radically separated as the material order and the spiritual order, to be really united?

God withdrew within himself; he took counsel as it were, according to the beautiful indication of Scripture, and in presence of all that was accomplished, before the attentive heavens and trembling earth he

pronounced the last creating word; he said: FACIAMUS
HOMINEM—*Let us make man!* Man obeyed that voice
which should never more cease to give him life and
light. A being appeared participating in matter by
which he became united to the inferior world, and in
spirit by which he became united to the superior
world; at the same time body and soul, the body
acting with the soul and the soul with the body; not
as being two, but as one only; not as brother
and sister, but as one single personal being called by
the same name, man. In man the mystery of universal
unity was solved; placed in the lowest rank of the
ascending line of beings, and on the first step of the
descending line, concentrating in his personality all the
gifts of the mind and all the forces of matter, communicating by his wants with the arctic and antarctic poles
of things, the real centre of the creation—he, by his
presence, stamps upon it the seal of its unity, and with
unity the seal of perfection. Behold man; behold his
place and his glory; behold why all the great religious
scenes have been enacted upon the earth which he
inhabits and in the very bosom of mankind. Rationalism is greatly troubled about the importance which
man attributes to himself; it has not disdained to call
astronomy to its aid in order to deprive us of the
eminent position to which Providence has raised us,

The General Plan of Creation. 113

and, comparing the insignificance of our race and the inferiority of our planet with all the suns fixed in space, it is pleased to make of us the pigmies, not to say the abortions of the universe. Let us leave to rationalism these pitiable gratifications of apostacy; and, as we are not afraid of being kings because we are not alarmed by the duties of the throne, let us learn to measure greatness by the essence and functions of beings, and not by their size or material rapidity of motion. The earth, it is true, is not the astronomical centre of the world; it suffices for it to bear mankind—the real centre of creation.

It is thus that God has communicated to his work the metaphysical perfection with which he is endowed. As to intellectual perfection, the second term of his total perfection, it was naturally to be found in man and in the spirits superior to man, since all of them, by their very essence, are capable of knowing. Matter alone, relegated to the frontiers of nothingness, seemed shut out for ever from the glorious privilege of thought. For God himself cannot accomplish that which includes an express contradiction, and matter, an inert and divisible substance, rejects, with all the force of an absolute incompatibility, the idea of activity indivisible as thought, free as the will. But God, without performing an impossibility, performed a miracle. He willed then to spiritualise matter, according to the expression of St. Paul, by giving it a share in the most elevated functions of the human soul, and this is the secret which was faintly perceived by Aristotle, when he said : " There is nothing in the intelligence which was not before in the senses." Not that the soul does not receive, prior to all intercourse between itself and nature, a direct illumination from God, an illumination which is to its inner vision what light is to the outer eye ; but, notwithstanding that divine communication, thought does not take its form, and, so to say, its outline, until the senses, by means of images and language, have brought to the soul, in its inmost sanctuary, the tribute of their exploration in the visible world. Man thinks only by means of the totality of his being, as he lives only by means of the totality of his being. All idealist or materialist systems are false, because they divide man by making him a simple intelligence or only a body. Man, in all his operations, is neither a body nor a spirit ; he is man, that is to say, that marvellous unity resulting from two substances intimately interwoven, the material substance and the immaterial substance. Everything that separates these destroys man.

Thus matter is raised to an incomprehensible state of dignity. Contemplate that unnamed dust at your feet, which is the last degree of abasement that being reaches before your eyes. Contemplate it. You bore it along but just now without deigning to notice it; a puff of air will cast it into a field; darkness and light embody it in the frail tissue of a plant. It is already wheat. The same chance that cast it under your feet brings it upon your table in its new form. You recognise it no longer, and yet it will soon become a part of yourself. See, it flows in your veins; it penetrates the tissues of your body; it mounts even to the supreme seat of your exterior activity, to that calm and elevated throne, where, under the protection of a powerful shield, the purest elements of life are silently elaborated. There it encounters the reciprocal action of the soul and the body; it comes between them; it knocks at the august portal of your intelligence; it helps you to think, to will; it is yourself, and yet it is the grain of dust under your feet.

I was then justified in calling St. Paul to bear witness to the grandeur of the world even in its lowest element. What if I were to advance yet further—if I pronounced to you that famous phrase: *The Word was made flesh?* If I showed you dust in its eternal wedlock with God? But let us not rob the future to serve the present; let us leave a shadow upon the Thabor of truth, and terminate this discourse by showing you how God has communicated his moral perfection to the world.

The moral perfection of God is resumed in two words: justice and goodness. In order for the world to receive its communication, it was not enough that man and the superior spirits were endowed with the double faculty of knowing and willing, of knowing good and realising it—another gift was needed, that of choosing between good and evil. For, without that free choice, what, in them, would justice or goodness have been? A necessary perfection stripped of all personal merit, which would have made of their life a succession of acts irresistibly ordered and accomplished. Now in God, whose total perfection was to be reproduced, that fatality does not exist. God is a free being. Naturally held in the immutable order of his essence, he acts without in full liberty; he creates or he does not create, he gives in the time and measure determined by his sovereign will; and even when he remains within his necessary operations, such as the relations of the three divine persons, he is subject to nothing exterior to himself. He is neither commanded nor necessitated. If, on the contrary, man and pure spirits had no choice between God and themselves, between the infinite and the finite, their personality would exist only as an absolute dependence upon the divine personality; they would be others and not themselves. They would not give themselves from justice or goodness, but from subjection to an empire foreign to their own deliberation. They would be deprived of moral perfection, because they would possess a morality totally inamissible, and consequently impersonal.

In God, it is true, morality is inamissible, but it is so without being impersonal, because it is not the action of another that subjugates the divine will, whilst in the creature deprived of free will it would be the infinite who oppressed the finite. The human will would become absorbed in the divine will.

It is needless to add that matter itself, raised to the state of humanity, shares, by its association with the soul, the honours of free will, and that it thus enters into participation of the rights and perils of the moral order. You will have already drawn this conclusion if my words have but thrown a little light upon the ways of divine wisdom in communicating to the world its triple and adorable perfection.

The consequence of perfection is beatitude. God is infinitely happy, because he is infinitely perfect. Having then called the world to enjoy his perfection, he should also have called it to enjoy his beatitude; and as beatitude terminates all in God, it is also necessarily the final term of creation for every being who has not been unworthy of his destiny. Here I touch the Gordian knot of truth, and I venture to believe that you have severed it yourselves. You will not ask me why God has not given beatitude without conditions of merit ; if I am not deceived, you know the reason. If, indeed, God had willed to communicate to the world all his properties, he should have communicated them in the order in which he himself possesses them, and in the only order in which it was possible for him to communicate them all. Now, the divine properties are simply perfection and beatitude ; perfection, the cause of beatitude ; and beatitude, the effect of perfection. If God had changed the order, in plunging us by the sole act of our birth into the possession of himself, whence his felicity springs, he would have deprived us of the first of his properties, which is perfection. For, as we have seen, free will is a necessary element thereof, which the direct and beatific vision of God would not have permitted us to possess, even for a single instant. Lost at the moment of our birth in the abyss of an infinite attraction, we should have offered to divine goodness no representation of his own liberty, no virtue, no merit, no return worthy of his gratuitous and liberal dispensation towards us. God owed it then to us and

The General Plan of Creation. 119

to himself to retard our beatitude in favour of our perfection. But to retard it was to hide himself for a time from created beings, to clothe himself before them in the veil of finite things, in order that, choice being possible to them, trial should be also possible with choice, and that from trial there should spring up within them justice worthy of praise, goodness worthy of love.

Thus the world was given possession of a sovereignty which placed it with glory in presence of God. Thus, having God for principle and end, it should gravitate towards him by a voluntary and grateful perfection, even to the day when, the entire orbit of its trial being achieved, it will repose in the bosom of God himself in a degree of beatitude equal to its fidelity.

I have traced for you the whole plan of Creation. I have shown you the materials employed therein, the ordinance they received, the reasons of that ordinance, and already knowing your beginning, you have learned to know your end. Your end and your beginning do not differ; God is your father, and God is also your end. He is the *Alpha* and the *Omega* of your destiny; you cannot look lower without losing yourselves, rise less high without perishing. In vain, being ungrateful, will you appeal to his goodness against his justice. I have just destroyed that hope by showing you in goodness itself the root of your duties. It is doubtless goodness that said: *Come, ye blessed of my Father, possess you the kingdom prepared for you from the foundation of the world.*[4] But it is also goodness that said: *Be you therefore perfect, as also your heavenly Father is perfect.*[5] For the natural movement of goodness is to communicate its properties, and God having only his perfection and his beatitude, the effect of the divine goodness is to communicate both to you in the same order in which they are in himself. If you refuse perfection because it exacts sacrifice from you, at the same time you refuse beatitude, which is its consequence. That order does not depend upon God; it is his proper and rigorous nature; the very nature of goodness of which justice is but the sanction.

[4] Matt. xxv. 34. [5] Matt. v. 48.

MAN AS AN INTELLIGENT BEING.

My Lord,—Gentlemen,

We already know the two terms of the mystery of destinies; we know what is our principle and our end. But that knowledge, all-important though it be, is far from being sufficient for us. It is a great thing to be assured that God is the source from whence we spring, that our end is to attain to his perfection and beatitude; it remains, however, for us to be directed upon that perilous road of which God occupies the two extreme points; for if we are unacquainted with its secrets, we are in danger of going astray in our very way, and of descending towards death instead of advancing towards him from whom proceeds all life, all perfection, all felicity. Where is then the road which we ought to follow? Is it traced out? Is it known with certainty?

You cannot doubt about it; God, who has revealed to us our principle and our end, must also have revealed to us the means of proceeding from one to the other, otherwise the object he had in view, which was to satisfy his goodness by communicating himself to his creatures, would not have been realised. Here we quit the universe in order to concentrate our attention upon man in particular; for it is man who first interests us, and moreover, in seeking the paths which God has opened to us that we may mount towards him, we unceasingly encounter the rest of creation either disputing the passage with us or opening it before us; and the theology of man, in virtue of the unity that co-ordains and combines every part of the divine work, will constantly blend with the theology of the universe. But man himself, within his proper nature, is an infinitely complex being. By his thought, he belongs to the intellectual order; by his will, to the moral order; by his union with his fellow-creatures, to the social order; by his body, to the physical order; by his entire soul, to the religious order: and, under all these relations, he has received means of attaining his end, which is perfection and beatitude. It is needful then, in order completely to unfold his destiny, to study man himself, and successively as an intelligent, moral, social, physical, religious being; and

Man as an Intelligent Being. 123

under these divers aspects to take account of the roads which eternal wisdom has prepared for him, and in which he must walk in order to avoid perishing. The course will be long; it will embrace not only the remaining conferences of this year, but all those which will follow even to the last day in which God may permit me to instruct you. In a word, the principle and the end of man being known to us, nothing remains in the development of doctrine but to expose to you, in all their historical and dogmatic course, the means given to man to attain his end.

I enter at once upon this subject, and man as an intelligent being will form my exordium.

Intelligence is the faculty of knowing. To know, is to see that which is; and to see that which is, is to possess truth; for truth is no other thing than that which is, inasmuch as it is perceived by the mind. Whence it results that truth is the object of the intelligence, and that the function of the intelligence is to seek, to penetrate, to retain truth; to live by truth, and for truth; this is its perfection and its beatitude. In the first place, it is its perfection; for the mind out of truth is in the state of ignorance or error; it sees not or sees badly, and in either case it is deprived of its object and function. It is like an eye which looks without seeing, or which sees that which has no reality;

an organ useless and dead in the first case, a false and dangerous instrument in the second.

But if truth be the perfection of the intelligence, it may be said without further proof that it is also its beatitude. For the one is the inevitable consequence of the other. As soon as a faculty is united to its object, as soon as it accomplishes its mission, it attains a state of repose because it attains its object ; a glorious repose, because it is legitimate ; full of joy, because it has been produced by God according to the pattern of his own operations, wherein all ends in transport. Therefore, in receiving the light of truth, the intelligence reposes, rejoices, exults ; in fine, is happy according to the nature of the vision that enlightens and fills it. Daily we experience this beatification of the understanding. Even in the lowest regions of nature there is no being or phenomenon, how imperceptible soever it may be, how indifferent soever it may appear, the discovery of which does not cause us a kind of magic transport. You all know the history of that great geometrician who, after having long battled with a problem that arrested his genius, all at once penetrated its secret whilst he was in a bath. Forgetting himself, he rose, and, the folly of enthusiasm depriving him even of the consciousness of his nudity, he ran through the streets of Syracuse, exclaiming :

I have found it! I have found it! This is the living image of those holy nuptials between the mind and intelligible light, when man has shown himself worthy of that immaterial alliance by a life which lessens the subjection of his double nature to the inferior order. Those blissful joys depend together upon the greatness of the mind and the greatness of the ideas that inundate it; they blend with the shores of the intelligence and the luminous course which flows between them.

Sometimes the mind is great without the light being also great; then come those times of mysterious sadness whose traces you may have observed on the generous brows of many of your contemporaries. Victims of doubt, they have drunk from the cup of knowledge without drinking from the cup of truth. They have studied past ages, interrogated the seas, followed the orbit of the heavenly bodies, nothing has escaped the perspicacity of their meditations, and yet a veil has remained before them which hinders them from thoroughly fathoming what they see, and from taking account of the illuminations of their own life. Light itself is darkness to them; each new discovery opens to them a new abyss; and like the labourer ploughing in the fields of Thebes or Babylon, who constantly strikes against unaccountable ruins, these mighty investigators of worlds, at each furrow which they trace in the immensity of things, raise up, even from the very bosom of science, great and painful obscurities. They have neither the peace of ignorance nor the peace of error; they see too much not to know, too little to understand, and however great may be the crime that hides truth from them, they have at least the honour of being unhappy because they do not possess it.

But after these long torments of doubt, if the veil be at last drawn aside, then the intelligence receives one of those vibrations whose voluptuous pain no tongue can describe. Then Augustine rises, and, for the first time, finding even friendship irksome, he withdraws to give current to his feelings in a torrent of solitary tears. He, who was lost in the vain love of glory and creatures, sees all the charms that deceived his youth vanish in a moment. Truth enraptures him; the azure plains of Lombardy, the hopes of renown, the most tender professions of erring hearts, have no longer any power to move him; he departs, leading his aged mother by the hand, and already from the port of Ostia he sees the obscure solitude which he thinks will hide him for ever from the admiration of the world as from the dreams of his past life. Tears of great men, heroic sacrifices, virtues born in a single hour, and which ages cannot destroy, you teach us the price of truth! You prove that it is indeed the perfection and beatitude of the intelligence!

Therefore one of the most formidable crimes is that of betraying and labouring against truth; for it is to betray our highest good, to strike us at the very height from whence our glory and felicity descend. What is man without intelligence, and what is intelligence without truth? If you deprive man of intelligence, he is nothing more than the dethroned king of the animal world; if, leaving intelligence to him, you withhold from him the gift of truth, you dig out for him an abyss as deep as the infinite; you prepare for him a torment of hunger never to be appeased, an aspiration which can never attain to anything but grasping shadows in an immense and deceptive void. What can be more terrible than this condition! What more criminal than to be its willing instrument! Therefore, falsehood has ever been abhorred by the human race; and, even in things where its insignificance would seem excusable, it brings infallible scorn upon the lips which give it utterance. We do not forgive the man who, knowing truth, willingly substitutes for it the adulterous language of error. How much less will God and mankind pardon those who designedly stand up against the most holy doctrines that ages have bequeathed to us, and who, despairing of conquering them by calm discussion, arm themselves against them with all the resources of violence and cunning! This has too often been witnessed, and we must never lose an opportunity of protesting against those pusillanimous conspiracies of might; the powers instituted for the conservation of all rights and possessions have been seen to declare open war against the highest of all rights, the right to know; against the richest of all possessions, namely, truth. Jealous of its power, which, indeed, is the greatest known in the world, they strive to dethrone it, in order to set up in its place and to their own profit the reign of interests and passions. Anything suits them better than truth; they accept, protect, give liberty to everything but truth. They pursue truth so exclusively, with so much art and perseverance, that they make it known by that same sign, and their very persecution becomes a mark of certainty which presents it to the legitimate adorations of the whole earth.

But do not wonder if truth some day or other takes vengeance upon its oppressors. As men are not able to ruin authority without striking at the root of the human understanding, sooner or later a kind of frenzy urges them beyond all fear and respect, and drives them with open arms against that which is. This is the time of reprisals, the time foretold by St. Paul when he wrote thus to the Romans:—*The wrath of God is revealed from Heaven against all ungodliness and injustice of those men who detain the truth of God in injustice.*[1] Then kings grow pale and kingdoms are troubled; night gathers in Babylon; Baltazzar sees the hand that condemns him, and the sword of Cyrus waits not for to-morrow. I am not reciting history; no, it is not history. Look around you; we are in Babylon, we sit at the feast of Baltazzar![2]

Must I ask your indulgence if I have allowed myself to yield to the emotions of a time so fertile in great lessons? Have I betrayed the interests of truth by showing you, in the catastrophes of our age, the avenging part which truth plays therein? If it be so, may you and truth forgive me, and let us remount together to the peaceful regions where nothing earthly disturbs the contemplation of causes and laws.

I have just proved that truth is the perfection and beatitude of the intelligence; and, since God in creating us has willed to communicate to us perfection and beatitude, I draw therefrom this consequence, that he has communicated truth to us. And it is, in fact, what Catholic doctrine teaches. If we listen to it, it teaches that God in sending us into the

[1] Rom. i. 18.   [2] A.D. 1848.

world did not abandon our mind to the hazard of its own discoveries, but enlightened it from the beginning with such knowledge that truth really existed therein. What was that primitive knowledge which, without being infinite, was nevertheless truth? That question leads us back to the definition which I gave you on commencing this Conference. Truth, I said, is that which is, inasmuch as it is perceived by the mind. We halted there without advancing that other question, which we can no longer avoid. What, then, is that which is? Do we understand by this the heavens, the earth, and the seas? Is this that which is? What? the heavens, the earth, the seas, mankind even, all that we see, is stamped with such a character of limit and change that we find there nothing of the grandeur contained in that powerful word—being: human tongues have exhausted their energies to express the nothingness of visible things, and however pride may desire to magnify the theatre upon which it acts, all that it can add to the universe is to discover in it a ray of being, and consequently a ray of truth. Where then is being? Where is that which is? Ah, already I perceive, and even know it. Being is absolute, eternal, and infinite unity, plurality without division, the ocean without shores, the centre without circumference, the plenitude that contains itself, the form without figure; the whole, in fine, without which all that is, is but an act and a gift. But in so speaking whom have I named? I have named him who has said of himself, EGO SUM QUI SUM—*I am who am*.³ I have named him who said also, EGO SUM VERITAS—*I am the truth*.⁴ I have named God. Behold being, and behold truth. God alone is truth, because he alone is being; he does not possess truth as something foreign to himself, but he is substantial and personal truth, because he is being, possessing himself; because he is at the same time, and by the same act, the eye that sees, the object seen, and vision. Whoever knows him knows all; whoever knows him not knows nothing. What know you indeed out of him? The phenomena of the world, their laws, the composition and decomposition of bodies, the science of dust. You do not even reach so far; for, to attain to this, you must at least penetrate the last reason of an atom, and where will you find it if you ignore God, the principle and the end of all?

From thence come those lamentations of the greatest minds about the poverty of science, lamentations so eloquently expressed by Solomon, one among them, when he said—*I have seen all things that are done under the sun, and behold all is vanity and vexation of spirit.*⁵

[3] Exodus iii. 14.   [4] John xiv. 6.   [5] Ecclesiastes i. 14.

Man as an Intelligent Being.

It is, in fact, because truth is not under the sun, it is above; it is in God, without whom man knows nothing, neither earth, nor heaven, nor present, nor future, nor man, nor even his own heart. And the more he learns without God and out of God, the more he enlarges, with the circle of his investigations, that of his doubts and torments. On the other hand, the man to whom God is revealed finds himself at the same moment in the centre and at the circumference of things; he sees their initial germ, their development, their term, their reason; if he knows nothing of the detail, he measures the whole, and his mind peacefully reposes in the double joy of knowledge and certainty. In a word, God, being truth, is the proper object of our intelligence, he is its perfection and beatitude; and when I said to you but now, that from the first he had given to us the gift of truth, I said that from the first he had revealed himself to us.

I find a beautiful confirmation of this in the first page of the Gospel of St. John—*There was*, says the Evangelist, *a man sent from God, whose name was John. . . . . He was not the light, but was sent to give testimony of the light. That was the true light which enlighteneth every man that cometh into this world.* If indeed there exist a supreme light, mother of all minds, its first act, when they come into the world, should be to enlighten them, and it can enlighten them only by making known to them their principle, which is God ; their end, which is God ; truth, which is God. If it failed to do this, what means would they have of accomplishing their destiny by tending towards their end? They would have none. And thus truth is not only due to them by right of the perfection and beatitude of the intelligence, it is due to them also as the first and necessary means, without which, being ignorant even of the object of their life, it would be impossible for them to advance towards that object, still more impossible to attain it. It is then with justice that Catholic doctrine makes truth— that is to say, the knowledge of God—one of the primitive gifts of man, the starting point, and I shall add, the milestone of his destiny.

To this, what does rationalism oppose ? You shall hear.

Eighteen hundred years ago a Roman proconsul called a prisoner before him, and after having attentively examined him as a man whose appearance was remarkable, he spoke to him these few words : *Thou art the King of the Jews?* The accused replied : *My kingdom is not of this world. If my kingdom were of this world my servants would certainly strive that I should not be delivered to the Jews ; but now my king-*

dom is not from hence. The proconsul continued: *Art thou a king, then?* The accused answered: *Thou sayest that I am a king. For this end was I born, and for this cause came I into the world, that I should give testimony to truth.* The proconsul stood up and said : *What is truth?*[6] This terrible question is the same that rationalism even now addresses to us whenever we speak of the basis of all faith and knowledge. Like the Roman, it asks : What is truth? And it must ask this question under pain of not protesting against the very foundation of the whole religious edifice, which is the idea of truth in itself. Now how could rationalism avoid protesting up to this point? How could it permit truth to affirm itself without being contradicted? How could it refrain from digging out under truth an abyss as deep as itself, and from making of the intelligence a faculty without certainty and without any other object than that of an incomprehensible enigma? It would be too weak on the part of rationalism, or too disinterested. It has not committed this fault, it has advanced straight to the question that precedes all others, and whilst the universe proclaims the works of truth, ages repeat its name, minds contemplate it, and its action is perpetuated by evidence and faith through the whole

[6] John xviii. 33, 36, 37, 38.

course of human generations, rationalism, opposing to that triumph the imperturbation of some of its sages, has boldly and fearlessly asked: What is truth? It has not denied; for to deny boldly is also to affirm. It has not said: There is nothing; but, Is there anything? It has not said: I know not; but, What do I know? In a word, it has raised up against absolute truth the icy arm of absolute scepticism.

Must we listen? Must we do so much honour to the reason which abdicates its throne, as to listen and reply? Yes, let us listen; let us learn how far intelligence afraid of God is able to annihilate itself from fear of adoring him. Scepticism reasons thus: Man sees in his mind something which he calls ideas, some, secondary and deduced, others, primordial without a generating principle, and which constitute the inscrutable foundation of his reason. All the ulterior conclusions of the understanding flow from this primary source, wherein analysis readily discerns the notions of being, unity, the infinite, the absolute, order, justice, which together take the august name of truth, or a still more august name, that of God. This is the fact. But because the mind possesses such ideas, does it follow that out of itself there are realities which correspond to them? It is not the mind itself which is being, unity, the infinite, the absolute, order, justice; nor does the mind directly perceive these. It sees but their shadow, if we may so speak, and the very word idea, in its origin, means only an image. But who can assure us that the image is exact, or even that it is produced by a real object? How can the intelligence, which is limited, be the mirror of the infinite? How, being contingent, relative, fallible, can it be the mirror of the necessary, the eternal, the just, the perfect? What proof have we that the ideal vision does not deceive us, and that it is any other thing than the permanent dream of a passing being? We believe that it is not so, but we believe this without demonstrating it, and we vainly endeavour to establish that demonstration; for every demonstration supposes principles upon which it is based, and these very principles of the understanding we have now to verify. Man encounters there an invincible obstacle; he may be able to ascend the Nile of his thought even to the elements which begin its course; beyond this, he becomes lost in a contemplation which renders to him but the sterile repetition of the ideas which he employs to enable him to advance further. The mind becomes an echo which answers to itself, and its voice appearing to it to come from a greater distance adds only an illusion to its powerlessness.

Man as an Intelligent Being. 137

I do not think that scepticism has said anything stronger than what you have just heard; it has perhaps said this in a more scientific manner, that is to say, in a more obscure manner, but not with more energy and sincerity. And I confess in the first place that it is impossible to demonstrate the primary ideas which form, as it were, the intimate substance of our reason. If they could be demonstrated, they would not be primitive; others would be so, and the same difficulties would arise in regard to them. We demonstrate only that which is a consequence, and not that which is a principle. Now our intelligence, being the faculty of a finite being, can be enlightened only by a transmitted light, a light which begins at a certain point and ends at another, a light which has a principle and an end. As principle, light is an axiom; as end, it is a mystery. Both of these, the axiom and the mystery, are indemonstrable, but the axiom is so on account of its clearness, the mystery on account of its obscurity. As the obscurity of the mystery is insurmountable, the clearness of the axiom is irresistible, and thus the understanding, at the two extremes of the horizon which it embraces, encounters a limit where its power is broken, or where its liberty ceases. It is powerless against the splendour of primary truths, and against the obscurity of final truths; it is exhausted before the former, and yields inevitably to the latter. This is why absolute scepticism is an effort against nature, which terminates only in self-deception, and in placing the actions of the man in perpetual contradiction with the reasonings of the sage. "If," said Pascal, "there is an impossibility of proving, which is invincible to all dogmatism, there is an impossibility of doubting, which is invincible to all pyrrhonism." We make no higher pretensions. For, what is certainty, but the impossibility of doubting? What is rational certainty, but the rapture caused by evidence which captivates the mind? Scepticism, it is true, stands up against the evidence of primordial ideas; it accuses this evidence of being purely subjective, that is to say, speaking so as to be understood, not attaining to a vision of the object which the ideas represent. But what matters it, if that evidence assures us naturally and invincibly of the reality of the things which the ideas represent. There is none but God, who—as being, unity, the infinite, the absolute, order, justice—confounds in his vision the subject and the object, the subject seeing and the object seen. For us who possess truth without being truth, we have no other natural means of beholding it and of being sure of its presence, than the light by which it appears to us, an intervening light which identifies itself with our minds, and which, seizing it as a part of itself, leaves it no other room for doubt than the resource of an act of suicide, so much the more powerless as it is never accomplished.

Indeed it may be said that there is nothing to reply to absolute scepticism; because there is nothing to reply to those who make objects of doubt of their ideas, their words, their very doubts. To reply, is to suppose a reality, were it only that of the objection. Now, as the sceptic destroys all reality, his objection becomes lost with him in the void which he hollows out for himself. It suffices to be silent before a shadow; to live before a dead body. So much the more as scepticism is but the malady of a small number of depraved minds, who, notwithstanding all the energy of their pride and all the glory of their aberrations, have never been able to escape from the chastisement of solitude. The generality of intelligent men have constantly disdained their sophisms, and believed with incorruptible faith in the reality of truth. What need you more? Error is something only by the adhesion of men; wherever mankind is not in a certain measure, nothing is left to error but a little noise in an empty tomb. It is a phantom which hopes to scare us, but the laugh of God and man render justice to it. This suffices for God and mankind; it is sufficient also for me.

If, however, absolute scepticism is but an unimportant chimera, it is not so of another kind of scepticism, which, attacking truth from a lower point, and not contesting its principal basis, produces a serious state of mind which it is necessary for us to notice. Absolute scepticism places in doubt the primitive notions that form the basis of human reason, and consequently the very idea of God; relative or imperfect scepticism gives its adhesion to these ideas, but refuses its faith to certain consequences which flow from them, and which embrace the nature of the divine acts. Absolute scepticism is atheism under a negative form; imperfect scepticism implies only an ignorance of the attributes and operations of God. It believes that God exists, but it does not take account of what he is, of what he does, or of what he wills to do. This is vulgar unbelief, and this very expression teaches us that it is no longer a question of a rare and chimerical condition, but a condition too real, in which man, so far from abdicating his intelligence, derives from it, on the contrary, forces for resisting truth, that is to say, God. Now God, we have said, manifests himself to man from his cradle, not in an incomplete manner, but to the full extent required by the need in which we stand of knowing our principle, our end, and the means of attaining it. How, then, should a certain portion of mankind be ignorant of God, or are they in a state of doubt with regard to him which hinders them from appreciating and accomplishing their true destinies? Is it the fault of man or the fault of God? It is needful for us to know this, in order that obscurities may not be left in your minds, which would be so much the more grievous, as it is now our object and yours that you may be instructed in the intellectual ways which God has opened to us that we may ascend towards him.

I repeat, then: Is that imperfect scepticism—such as I have defined it, and in which so many reasonable beings pine—the work of God or the work of man? Has God been sparing of light, or is it man who has retreated from it? In order to solve this question, we must seek to learn by what means and in what measure God primitively communicated truth to the human race.

Doubtless God could have shown himself to us face to face, in all the brightness of his essence, and, in this case, scepticism would never have appeared upon earth. Every veil being withdrawn, truth, which is but the divine nature, would have taken irrevocable possession of our intelligence. Intelligible light, instead of appearing to us between the axiom and the mystery, that is to say, with a principle and an end, would have risen for us in all the ineffable plenitude of its own immensity. Evidence would have been ecstacy, certainty would have taken the character of immutability, truth would have become the eternal life of our minds: But that state, so far from being our original state in the divine plan, was precisely the supreme term to which we were called. I have already told you for what reason. I have shown you, in exposing to you the general ordinance of the universe, that God, moved by his goodness, willed to communicate to us his perfection and beatitude, and that beatitude, given without the previous condition of free will, would have deprived us of the merit and glory of perfection. From whence it follows that a state of trial should precede the final state of beatification, and that state of trial, founded upon free will, necessarily included the possibility of believing or not believing, of admitting or rejecting truth, that is to say, the liberty of the understanding. Now, the liberty of the understanding was incompatible with a direct vision of the divine essence, and consequently it was needful that God should veil himself from our sight, and be for us at the same time a hidden God and a God known, hidden without envy, known freely.

But how are we to see that which is unseen? How are we to know that which does not fall directly under the eye of the mind? If this difficulty could not be solved, the plan of God in creation would be impossible to realise. Can it therefore be solved? God possessed in his double nature the pattern of a double vision, the intuitive vision and the ideal vision. Present to himself by the intuitive vision, he discovered by the ideal vision the things which he should one day create. These things evidently formed no part of his essence under their positive and realised form; he did not then behold them in himself under that substantial form; nor did he behold them out of himself before communicating to them the being which was wanting to them. Where then, and how, did he behold them, if not, as I have just said, by way of image, of representation, under that intelligible and mysterious form which we call an idea? St. Thomas of Aquinas proposes this question: "Are there ideas in God?" And he answers: "Yes; for as the world was not made by chance, but by the action of the divine intelligence, there must have pre-existed in the divine intelligence a form or likeness of the world, and that form or likeness is the idea itself."[7] Now, if God beheld the sensible world by the ideal vision, why did not man

[7] Summa, first part, question 15, art. 1.

see the divine world by the same kind of vision ? Why, without discovering the very substance of being, unity, the infinite, the absolute, order, justice—all of which things are God under different aspects and under different names—did he not receive the idea of him in his mind, and with the idea a distinct knowledge of him, worthy of being called truth ? Can we say that we do not understand what is being, unity, the infinite, the absolute, order, justice ? And if we do understand this, if this is the very torch that enlightens all the rest, what is within our soul and what is without, can we accuse God of not having enlightened us, of not having cast before our life the pale and uncertain light of visible things ? Yes, whilst hiding himself from us, that is to say, whilst leaving a veil upon the substantial fount of his being, God has fully given himself to us, by the exact impression of his likeness in the living flesh of our understanding. He has traced out in it luminous furrows, and with a generous hand has sown that incorruptible germ of truth which teaching, reflection, experience, and even the course of our years, unceasingly develope, so far as to cause us to attain, save by our own fault, to divine maturity ; to that glorious moment when the image of God, fully formed within us, bursts the envelope which covers it, and rejoins in immortality the ineffable type which was its father, and which recognises its son.

It is not then the want of light that precipitates a part of mankind into scepticism and keeps them away from truth, it is the abuse of their free will. The darkness wherein they lose God, is voluntary darkness; God shows himself, and they fly from him; God is the object present to their intelligence, and they choose to make of their intelligence a sepulchre or a chaos, rather than adore the star that shines upon it. They abandon that inner light, the only true light, to pursue the obscure and powerless attractions of the material universe, from which they expect the joy of apostacy in the pride of false science. And yet the universe, all limited as it is, all pale and silent as it rises before our minds, is itself full of God. If it be not his likeness, it contains at least a vestige, a lineament of him; from the hyssop to the cedar, from the dew of morning to the evening star, all nature is a reflection of the divine power, beauty, and goodness. God, who in the body of man has associated matter with the most subtle operations of the mind, has willed, in the body of the world, to associate it with the revelation which his mind perpetually makes to our own. To each ray of ideal light there corresponds a ray of sensible light; to each vision of the uncreated world, a vision of the created; to each voice of the one, the voice of the other. But man separates what God has united; enlightened by a double light, because of his double substance, he does not perceive that both meet in a single fount, as our double substance terminates in one single personality, and, dividing truth by a divorce which destroys it, he opposes the revelation from without to the revelation from within, nature to God, matter to spirit. Or at least he disdains the superior light, as a sort of vague apparition in a badly defined horizon, whilst he cleaves to the inferior light as to the only one which possesses a precise and positive character. From that moment, all that relates to God, his attributes, his acts, becomes obscured in that adulterous understanding; even if he does not descend to absolute scepticism, he clearly distinguishes only that which strikes the senses, and the true, in his eyes, is that alone which bears the stamp of a palpable and vulgar reality.

Are there then really more obscurities in the mind than in the body? Does the sensible world possess more clearness than the intelligible world? Is earth instead of heaven the great illuminator of man, and has God erred in the construction of our being so far as to have sacrificed the part which tends towards him to that which tends towards nothingness?

Man as an Intelligent Being. 147

You do not think so: Catholic doctrine affirms the contrary for us, and the most simple observation of the exercise of our faculties will show us that Catholic doctrine is in the right. Even natural science—that is to say, that which occupies itself only with the visible order—would be unable to subsist without employing notions which it draws from the invisible or metaphysical order. Despoil man of these fertile principles, take from him the ideas of being, unity, extent, force, relation, what would the universe be for him? Precisely what it would be for an animal—a spectacle. He would behold it without thinking about anything but beholding it; so far from penetrating its laws, he would not even have a confused presentiment of what a law is. A purely instinctive being, rendering to the world nothing superior to the world, he would stand mute before it, and his hand, which now leads the distant stars, would never beforehand have traced out for them the inevitable course which they unconsciously follow. It is the mind that sheds light upon the obscurity of nature; it is the mind that discovers the connection and the cause of phenomena; it is the mind that measures, calculates, analyses, defines, dictates orders to matter; in fine, that unravels in that labyrinth the thread left there by God, and by which he still holds it suspended to the will that created it.

But the mind without the idea is but an unlighted torch, and the idea without a germ sown from above, greater and clearer than all the worlds, is itself but the powerless reflection of nature upon a faculty which, possessing nothing, has nothing to respond thereto. In vain materialism tells us that sensation becomes an idea on falling into the intelligence; it is as if it said that limit on entering into void becomes infinite. Sensation, because of the intimate union between the soul and the body, may awaken the intelligible grain that reposes in the depths of the mind; it may draw it forth from a kind of solitary abstraction, which is not in relation with the constitution of a being at the same time spiritual and material: but it is impossible for it to give to the mind what it does not possess, or to receive from the mind that which itself had not. Two lights become strengthened by uniting; a ray of light does not become the sun by passing through darkness.

It is then by an abuse even of the forces of the intelligible and divine order, that man withdraws from the exalted regions of the mind to bury himself in the science of terrestrial phenomena. He draws from his intelligence treasures of knowledge and harmony; he scatters them with profusion upon the world; next, beholding it reinvested with that sublime beauty which he has made for it, he believes that it is the world which has enlightened him, that in it alone is full certainty, that it alone merits the honour of assiduous cultivation, and, banishing God to an inaccessible throne, he is not slow to lose sight of him, to forget him, to misunderstand him, to have no other notion left of him than a notion vague and profitless. Thus is imperfect scepticism formed from the voluntary predominance of the material order over the ideal order.

But there is another cause of this, about which I must not be silent, and the exposition of which will fully make known to you the means which God has employed to initiate our intelligence to the perfection and beatitude of truth.

In depositing within us the ideal or intelligible seed, in placing us by our senses in relation with the phenomena and laws of the universe, God enlightened us by a double revelation, the one interior, the other exterior. This was a great gift; but it was not to communicate himself to us personally, inasmuch as he is truth; had he remained there and given us nothing more, we should have known him only by means of nature and ideas, that is to say, indirectly. He willed to advance further, and, without however revealing to us his essence, to establish personal relations between our minds and his own. He spake to us then. It is a fundamental point of Catholic doctrine that a word of God was, from the very first, shed upon mankind, and that it has never ceased to exist and to spread in the world, either adulterated or in a pure state, as an immortal echo of truth; an echo often weakened, often corrupted, but rising again from its ruins through all generations, and recalling to us, with the eloquence of perpetuity, the existence of God, his nature, his acts; that he is the principle, the end, the means, the key of our destinies. Traditions, common to all nations and all ages, continually attest that oral revelation primitively made to the human race: human language itself, constantly transmitted by hereditary succession, and neither historically nor logically permitting the possibility of an origin by way of invention to be even perceived, bore testimony also to the reality of an anterior and a divine language, from whence our own issued. In the forests man has been found lowered to the rank of animals, from a precocious abandonment which had deprived him of all teaching. Language from his lips was nothing more than a vague, an inarticulate sound, a barbarous cry indicating the presence of sensations and incapable of transmitting ideas. All these facts confirm the page of Scripture which shows God speaking with man; and by the effusion of oral light achieving that which the gift of intelligible and sensible light had commenced within him. But it was reserved for our epoch to acquire from that truth a demonstration as marvellous as it was unlooked for.

Towards the end of the last century, a French priest, touched by the misfortunes of those poor creatures who are born deprived of speech because deprived of hearing—a circumstance which again bears witness to the close connection between the mystery of language and the mystery of a previous instruction—a priest, I say, touched by the condition of the deaf and dumb, devoted his life to leading them out of their sad solitude, by seeking an expression of thought which might reach their own and succeed in drawing from their bosoms, so long closed, the secret of their inner state. He attained this object. Charity, more ingenious than misfortune, had the happiness of opening the issues which nature held closed, and of pouring, into these obscure and captive souls the ineffable, although imperfect, light of speech. The benefit was great, the recompense was still greater. As soon as these unknown intelligences were penetrated, investigation discovered in them nothing resembling an idea. I do not speak only of a moral and religious idea, but of a metaphysical idea. Nothing was found there but an image of what falls under the investigation of the senses, there was nothing of what falls from a higher region into the mind. Sensation was caught here in the very fact of powerlessness. What do I say, sensation?—the intelligence itself, although endowed with the ideal seeds of truth, although assisted by the revelation of the sensible world, the intelligence appeared in the deaf and dumb in a state of sterility. Men, already ripe in years, born in our civilisation, who had never quitted it, who had been present at all the scenes of family and public life, who had seen our temples, our priests, our ceremonies, those men being interrogated on the intimate working of their convictions, knew nothing of God, nothing of the soul, nothing of the moral law, nothing of the metaphysical order, nothing of any one of the general principles of the human mind. They were in a purely instinctive state. The experiment has been repeated a hundred times, and a hundred times it has produced the same results ; and hardly do we perceive, in the multitude of documents published up to this time, a doubt or a difference of opinion on so capital a fact, which is the greatest psychological discovery the history of philosophy can boast of. Has thought then received in language an auxiliary so indispensable that, without its help, man was condemned to incapability of emerg-

Man as an Intelligent Being. 153

ing from the reign of sensations? Was language, for all the operations of the intelligence, the point or means of junction between the soul and the body? Did our double nature require that sort of incarnation of what is most immaterial in the world, or had God willed to make us comprehend the dependency of our mind by rendering it incapable of becoming fertile without the exterior action of oral instruction?

Whatever may be the explanation of this, it has always been found certain that man does not speak before he has heard language, and that he thinks only after the ideas contained in language have awakened the intelligible germ deposited in the depths of his understanding. If he did not possess this intelligible germ, language, in passing through the organs of his hearing, would vainly solicit his intelligence; he would hear it only as a sound, and not as a living expression of truth. But truth pre-exists in him in the same manner as the tree pre-exists in its seed and as the consequence pre-exists in its principle. Just as after-teaching causes to bud forth within each of us an innumerable multitude of deductions included in primary ideas, but of which our mind had no consciousness, so initial teaching causes the primary ideas themselves to appear to our inner vision. You find it natural that language should reveal to you mathematics, although you possess them entire in the primordial notions of unity, number, extent, weight: why does it appear strange to you that language should cause you also to perceive notions of unity, number, extent, weight, which are the base of mathematics? One of these phenomena is not more remarkable than the other; perhaps even it is more easy to understand the integral and profound sleep of a faculty which nothing analogous to it had yet disturbed, than to understand why that faculty, once called into exercise, halts in its way, and waits for language to manifest to it the simple consequences of what it clearly sees. The fact, however, remains incontestable, and that language is always the primitive and necessary motor of our ideas, as the sun, in agitating by his action the vast extent of air, produces there the brilliant scintillation which gives light to our eyes.

Thence it follows that Catholic doctrine is true when it exhibits to us God teaching the first man, whether in causing the truth of his intelligence to emerge by the percussion of the verb, or in announcing mysteries to him which surpassed the forces of the purely ideal order, as we shall by and by perceive. In fact, since man thinks and speaks only after having heard others speak, and since, on another hand, human generations take their beginning in God, their creator, it follows that the first movement of language and thought remounts to the hour of creation, and was given to man, who possessed nothing, by him who possessed all, and who willed to communicate all to him. This movement once impressed, intellectual life began for the human race, and has never since ceased. The divine word, immortalised upon the lips of man, has spread like an inexhaustible stream divided into a thousand branches through the vicissitudes of nations, and preserving its force as well as its unity in the infinite mixture of idioms and dialects, it perpetuates in the very seat of error the generating ideas which constitute the popular fund of reason and religion. If human liberty vitiates its teaching, it is but in a limited manner; its efforts do not attain so far as to reach the lowest depths of truth. Language, by that alone that it is pronounced, bears in its essence a light which seizes the soul and renders it an accomplice, if not in all, at least in the fundamental principles without which man altogether disappears. Therefore, God, by the effusion of his word continued in our own, does not cease to promulgate the gospel of reason, and every man, whatever he may do, is the organ and missionary of that gospel. God speaks in us in spite of us; the mouth that blasphemes still contains truth; the apostate who renounces him still makes an act of faith, the sceptic who mocks at all employs words that affirm all.

However, if absolute scepticism is powerless against the revelation of language, it is not the same with imperfect or vulgar scepticism, which does not disavow human reason, but contests only certain applications of it relative to the superior order which does not fall under the investigation of our senses. This kind of scepticism rejects in particular all personal relation between God and us by means of language; and maintains that our ideas spring of themselves from the living sources of the understanding, and in supposing that language may be necessary to their intimate emission, does not recognise in that marvellous functionary any traditional and divine character. God has not spoken to man; man has spoken of himself. He is the son of his own works, and all that he possesses of truth he owes to the success of his own investigations.

I have refuted this system, which is the cornerstone of rationalism, and which explains to you the blindness wherein so many creatures destined to know and love God live far from him. God has given light to us under three forms, which are perfected by each other—the intelligible form; the sensible form; the oral or traditional form. Now rationalism admits only the two former, and rejects with tradition the invincible certainty found in the dogmas affirmed by God. It opens to its adepts the field of unlimited speculation, to which the best disposed bring but an imperfect intelligence, obscured by prejudices of birth and education, still more dangerously vitiated by the domination of the senses over the mind. But were all these obstacles surmountable, there would still remain the greatest of all, namely, the order established by God in the communication of truth which he has made to man. If man were a pure spirit, he would see truth in intelligible light, without the help of any sensible element. If, being unity composed of body and soul, he had not been destined to hold personal relations with God, he would probably have seen truth in the combination of intelligible and sensible light, independently of all oral tradition. But he is at the same time spirit and matter, and in addition he is called to live in society with God; and this is why truth has been communicated to him under a mode which is triple and single, corresponding to his nature and vocation. Would he think as an angel thinks? He cannot; some exterior image always intervenes in his most subtle operations. Would he think as an animal? He is equally unable;

the height of his speculations elevates him even in the act by which he degrades himself, and even in concluding that he is only matter he proves that he is spirit. In fine, would he think like a being separated from God, independent of all personal relation with him, supported by his reason alone? Doubtless he can do this, but only by losing at the same moment the equilibrium of his intelligence; he seeks, he hesitates, he deceives himself, and even when he touches truth, the clouds that cover it and the horizon that limits it take from him the hope of lifting by himself alone the immense weight of earth and heaven. The history of the human mind offers on every page superabundant proof of this. Two systems of philosophy dispute for empire—religious and traditional philosophy, and rationalist or critical philosophy. The first, even when it is mixed up with errors, settles minds and founds nations; the second, even when it affirms a portion of truth, destroys what the other builds up.

In a word, God, who is truth, has made himself known to us by three revelations which are but one, by ideas, by the universe, and by language. Whoever breaks the bond that unites these, confuses and divides the light that lightens every man coming into the world; he condemns himself to a state of ignorance which knowledge does but increase; he will live at hazard like a being without principle or end, because he will voluntarily have abdicated, with truth, that is to say, with the knowledge of God, the highest means given to us to accomplish our destiny—which is to tend towards God, and, by imitating him, to obtain the perfection of his nature and the beatitude of his eternal life.

MAN AS A MORAL BEING.

MY LORD,—GENTLEMEN,

MAN is not simply an intelligence, he is not simply a contemplative being. If God had given him only the activity of contemplation, his life would have been limited to a simple and perpetual vision, to an impassible adoration of truth. But man is also an affective and an operative being; he is endowed with a second faculty, which is the consequence of the first, and has two acts, one expressed by the words: I love ; the other by: I command. This faculty is the will. We have then to learn what God did for the will when he created man, and what means he has com municated to us, in and by the will, for attaining ou end, which is perfection and beatitude.

But before entering upon this grave subject, gentlemen, I have two requests to address to you. I pray you first, never to applaud me, whatever may be the sentiment that moves your hearts. Not that I do not comprehend the involuntary movement which, even at the feet of the altars, causes an assembly to stand up, so to say, in unanimous witness of its sympathy and its faith. But although on certain occasions these acclamations might appear excusable, so much do they spring with piety from the souls of an auditory, nevertheless I conjure you to respect the constant tradition of Christendom, which is to respond to the word of God only by the silence of love and the immobility of respect. You owe this to God; you owe it also perhaps to him who speaks to you in his name. Although he may not have been tempted into pride by your applause, he may be suspected of not being insensible to it; it may be supposed, that, instead of giving freely to you that which he has freely received, he comes to seek its price in the glory of popularity, a recompense sometimes honourable, but always fragile, and still more fragile, more vain, between those who receive and him who gives the lessons of eternity.

The second request I would address to you is in favour of a nation to which on more than one occasion, and even from this place, I have already proved my respectful attachment. Yesterday, three noble sons of

Poland visited me; they told me that four thousand of their companions, after fifteen years of exile, were about to approach their country, with the consent of France, which opens to them her gates, and of Germany, which permits them to pass through her territory. They asked me, after having obtained permission from the chief of this diocese, here present, to beg of you in their name, a last proof of your pious fraternity; for, if time has respected their glory and not lessened their courage, it has left them those precious remains, and nothing more. I bent before their desire as before their misfortune; I present them to you together. You will not give them alms; for although that word is dear to your Christian hearts, there are times when the heroism of misfortune constrains you to seek a higher title. You will not pay them tribute; although that word supposes a debt, and a debt of an important character, yet it does not sufficiently express the unction of Christian language. Therefore, borrowing a celebrated expression of the middle ages, I ask you to give them a viaticum, that is to say, the travelling pay given in those times to the members of religious orders and to the knights who went to combat in the Holy Land for the emancipation of Christendom. You will give a viaticum to those sons of another hallowed land, to those soldiers of another generous cause; you will give them the triple viaticum of honour, exile, and hope.

This said, this double satisfaction proposed to your heart and to my own, I enter at once upon the subject which claims your attention.

As truth is the object of the intelligence, good is the object of the will. But what is good? What distinction is there between the good and the true? Is it not the same thing under two different names? I grant that the good and the true have the same root, the same substantial support, since the true is being, and the good is also being. But as the unity of the divine essence does not exclude the triplicity of persons, the unity of being does not hinder it from possessing many aspects. In the first place, it is light; and under that form reveals itself to the intelligence, and is called truth. Next it is order, harmony, beauty; and under that form it seizes the will, and is called good. Our nature thus corresponds to its own. Inasmuch as it is light, we respond to it by a faculty destined to know the true; inasmuch as it is order, harmony, beauty, we respond to it by a faculty destined to reproduce good in loving and practising it. And as truth is the perfection and beatitude of the intelligence, good is the perfection and beatitude of the will.

In the first place it is its perfection; for outside of good all is evil, that is to say, disorder, confusion, deformity: and evidently the will which loves and produces disorder, confusion, deformity, is in a false or an unjust state, as, on the other hand, the will which loves and produces good, that is to say, order, harmony, beauty, is in a state of justice or perfection.

I add that good is also the beatitude of the will: for thereby and therein it produces the most powerful sentiment of man, that sentiment which moves and fills from its very depths the vast solitude of his soul. No doubt the joy of truth known is great; there is in the regard that encounters the splendour of the true a motionless thrill, almost ecstatic; but if it reach to ecstacy, to tears, be sure that the intelligence has not alone been touched, the vision has penetrated still further, man has received the supreme shock from on high, the touch of love which terminates all in itself as in God. In the intuition of truth, man did not emerge from himself, he regarded the light present to his mind, and entered into enjoyment of it as an element or a part of his proper personality. By the impulsion of love, he emerges from his own personality or his life; he seeks a foreign object, he attaches himself to it, he embraces it, he longs to be transformed and absorbed into another than himself. This rapture from self to self, which may be called an attempt at suicide, gives him a bound of unspeakable happiness, and the abandonment of his being becomes its plenitude. This is love. But what has caused him to love? What has been powerful enough to take possession of that being, and so to subject him as even to make him feel that death in another is the best and highest life? A power, gentlemen, has wrought this miracle, the power of good. Behind the light where being appears to him, or in that very light, man has seen order, harmony, beauty, and this spectacle drawing him from the sterile contemplation of his own excellence, he feels that he is led to divest himself of himself in order to live in the object of his vision.

Nothing is more familiar to us than this movement, of all those of our nature it is the most universal, the most common, and that which we most willingly push to extravagance. Our life is passed in undergoing or regulating it. Every being possessing a certain amount of good, that is to say, endowed with order, harmony, and beauty in a certain measure, there is not one which is not capable of exciting within us some impression of love. But from man to man especially that impression appears and increases. Man is here below the masterpiece of good. He draws to his noble form the charm of the two worlds to which he belongs, the world of bodies and the world of spirits. Superior in the ordering of his features even to the imagination, which has never been able to conceive anything more perfect, he also calls to them from the depths of his soul the reflection of thought and the expression of virtue. If he open his eyes, a spirit looks at you; if his lips are left silent, the grace of the heart animates in closing them; if serenity brighten his forehead, the peace of an upright conscience sheds upon it light and repose; every bend of his body, every movement of his life contains under a single expression of beauty the double empire of visible and ideal good. Thence come those attachments which make of human life a long course of sacrifices rewarded by the happiness of loving and being loved. We do not seek elsewhere the secret of being happy; we know that it is there, and even when we abuse it by culpable passions, in the very crime we still bear witness to that law of our nature. Should man refuse us the love which we need, rather than renounce that precious treasure, we shall seek it from beings placed beneath us, but distantly preserving in their instinct some likeness capable of beguiling our heart. The poor man who has no other friend, makes one of some creature more neglected than himself; he warms in his bosom that obscure and faithful animal which a Christian writer has so well called the poor man's dog. He smiles upon him with that ineffable look of the forsaken; he confides to him those unknown tears which no tenderness wipes away; he shares his daily crust with him, and that sacrifice made by hunger to friendship causes him even in his poverty to enjoy the great happiness of riches, the happiness of giving.

Nor is this the last effort made by man to give and receive love. The prisoner goes beyond the poor. Separated from nature and mankind by inexorable barriers, he perceives in the chinks of his dungeon some lowly insect the imperceptible companion of his captivity. He draws near to it with the trembling emotion of hope and the delicacy of respect; he watches the mystery of its existence, marks its tastes, spends long days in teaching it not to fear him, in leading it from timidity to confidence, in order at last to obtain from it some reciprocal sign which will lessen the solitude of his heart and widen his prison walls. The dog consoles the poor, the spider melts the prisoner; man, the child of good, carries everywhere with him a love of it which turns into a resource and a joy even the very horrors of isolation.

Need I say more? Have not your souls passed beyond my words, and do you not see that good, real or apparent, disposes of our will and is its beatitude?

But what, then, is good? It is true I have already told you; I have said that good is the order, harmony, beauty, which the intelligence discovers in the light where being appears to it. Nevertheless, this definition, all exact though it be, is not the term where your minds halt. You desire a more profound explanation, you ask me where order, harmony, beauty are to be found?

Where? Doubtless everywhere in nature, everywhere before your eyes. There is not a leaf of the tree, not a blade of grass, not a cloud skimming the heavens, which is not order, harmony, beauty; but not all order, all harmony, all beauty, not all good. Every being, even the one perverted by his fault, contains a portion of good, which is perceptible and excites our sympathy; it does not contain the totality of good. That is order, which includes in its essence the rule from whence all the relations of beings proceed; that is harmony, which has weighed the worlds, and has traced out for them in space roads in which they never wander; that is beauty, which has made man, and stamped upon his visage so much grace and majesty; that is good, from whence all good comes, and which has shed it so profusely in the universe, without being able to give it all, because it could not give the infinite. Order, harmony, beauty, good, in one word, is God. As he is being and truth, he is also good. Inasmuch as he is being, he has communicated to us existence; inasmuch as he is truth, he enlightens our understanding; inasmuch as he is good, he inspires us with the love, which, according to the language of the Gospel, is all the law and all justice. For we can receive nothing greater, give nothing greater, than love; it is the supreme credit or debt, and whoever is quit towards it, is quit towards all. Now the first to whom we are accountable for it, the first who has a right to this highest treasure of our soul, is God, since God is the only good, and since good alone is the cause of love.

Whoever has not loved God is certain not to love good. He may, I grant, love particular things which are good, his family, his friends, his country, honour, and even duty, if we take duty in the narrow sense which governs the relations of men among themselves; he will not love the universal and absolute good from whence proceed all the other phases of good to which he has devoted his heart. And this is why he will not attain to the perfection and beatitude of the will, which, being in the love of good, can be found only in the love of God.

You see that in the mystery of love as well as in the mystery of truth, we arrive at the same conclusion, namely, that in God alone lies our perfection and our beatitude. And it is impossible that you should wonder at this, since we have established, as the foundation of doctrine, and as the knot of our destinies, that God is at the same time our principle and our end. Being our principle, he is the principle of each of our faculties; being our end, he is also the end of each of our faculties. And that end identifying itself with the divine perfection and beatitude, it is necessary for each of our faculties, by the way proper to it, to draw from God the life which renders it perfect and happy. Nevertheless, the developments through which I have led you are not sterile repetitions of the points of doctrine which we have before advanced and demonstrated; for, besides causing you to see their application to each of the springs of human activity, they verify those doctrines superabundantly by the analysis of our acts and of their objects. What joy do we not feel, in simply defining the intelligence and the will, on meeting God at the term of their operations! What ecstacy to be unable to name either truth or good, without naming God himself! And, in addition, those investigations lead us straight to the means which we must have

Man as a Moral Being.

received for attaining our end. Already, in the last Conference, we have proved that the first of these means is the knowledge of God; we are now prepared to conclude that the love of God is the second.

In fact, that love being the perfection and beatitude of our will, and God having designed to communicate the one and the other to us, as we have seen, it follows that, according to the order of his design, he should create us in a state of love with him; of initial love, it is true, subject to the trial of our free will, but preparing us and leading us, save prevarication on our part, to the final and beatific union of consummated charity. This is what Catholic doctrine teaches us, when it represents to us the first man being born in original charity or justice. Remark, I pray you, that beautiful alliance of expression; in Christian language, charity is the synonyme of justice, and justice is the synonyme of charity. I have just told you for what reason. Without that divine justice of love, man is separated from God, even in knowing him; and, being separated from him, he can but descend towards misery and death, by the road directly opposed to that into which the order of his creation calls him. According to that order, he has received God for his end, truth for his guide, charity for his motor. If he wander, it is not in default of means, but of will.

Here we again encounter the intervention of free will in our destinies, and, if its presence disturb you, I might limit myself to repeating that without free will the gifts of God would remain in us as we received them, with a character of fatality which would make of our perfection a work unworthy of God or of us. But this explanation, all sufficient though it be, calls for developments which would have been premature when we exposed to you the general plan of creation, and which are no longer so when we touch, in the question of the will, the foundations of the moral order. The will is the seat of free choice as well as of love; we love by the same organ which gives us the empire of our acts, and which, with that empire, imposes our personal responsibility. And these three things blended together, free will, love, and responsibility, are those which indivisibly constitute the moral order. Free will presents the choice, love chooses, man responds. Why is it so? Is it arbitrary wisdom that has enchained these three elements of our activity? Or is there some profound reason for this which it is our duty to penetrate, in order to illuminate with a final trait the mystery of God in the creation of this world?

You think I shall adopt the last conclusion; I do adopt it, and I ask that question which includes all the rest in itself: Is there any essential relation between love and free will which makes the one the condition of the other? To know this, it is necessary for us thoroughly to scrutinise love. It plays also so important a part in our souls and in Christianity, that we shall not regret the thoughtful regard which we shall have thrown upon its essence.

Nothing is more simple, more single, than love; and yet it includes three acts in the unity of its movement. In the first place, it is an act of preference. Man, however great his heart may be, cannot cleave alike to all; surrounded by objects which, in divers degrees, bear the stamp of good, he feels degrees in the attraction which inclines him towards them, sympathetic degrees, whose order does not solely depend upon the comparative goodness of the beings, but also upon their secret resemblances to ourselves. Often even we do not take account of the motives of our preference; what is certain is that we have preferences, and that love begins in us by that first movement, which is choice. What is also certain is that choice, in him who is its author, as in him who is its term, gives the impulsion to the elevated joys of love. We are happy in choosing, happy also in being chosen. Two beings meet in the immensity of time and space, through the numberless chances of creation; they meet as if they had given rendezvous to each other from all eternity; they are united by a reciprocal preference which honours both, and flatters in their pride that which is pure and venerable. Nothing surpasses the original charm of that instant which remains the first in our memory, as it was the first in our heart. After years have weakened other impressions, that still subsists in its serene youth, and carries us back to those happy days when we felt the glory of choosing and of being chosen. But what would choice be without free will? What would it be without the faculty of preferring what pleases us? Doubtless the motives of preference exist in the perfection of the being who is its object; but they exist also and equally in the will which makes the choice. It may despise, it may reject an excellence towards which it feels no sympathy, for another with which it corresponds, and herein consists the value of its act, a sovereign act which confers honour and produces joy only because it is sovereign.

Love, however, does not stop at the act of choice, it exacts devotedness to the being chosen. To choose is to prefer one being to all others; to be devoted is to prefer that being to ourselves. Devotedness is the immolation of self to the object loved. Whoever does not reach this point does not love. In fact, preference alone implies only an inclination of the soul which seeks to dilate in that which has caused it, an inclination honourable and precious, doubtless, but which, thus limited, results only in seeking itself in another. If many affections stop at this point it is because many affections are but disguised egotism; we feel an attraction, we yield to it, we think that we love, we have perhaps the glimmerings of real love; but when the hour for devotedness comes, the dread of sacrifice shows us the vanity of the sentiment which preoccupied without possessing us. We see frequent and lamentable examples of this in the passions which have for their principle the fugitive beauty of the body. Nothing intelligible and immortal intervening between the souls which yield to these sad seductions, their charm soon disappears in the very ardour which produced them, and they leave in the heart nothing but the devastations of egotism increased by deceptive enjoyments. Virtue alone produces love, because virtue alone produces devotedness. We see proof of this in all the affections in which virtue mingles the divine balm of its presence. It is virtue that inspires the mother bent night and day over the cradle of a child; it is virtue that inspires the breast of the soldier, and leads him on to death for the cause of his country; it is virtue that fortifies the martyr against the threats of tyrants, and causes him to recline in the tortures prepared for him as in the nuptial and joyful couch of truth. These are the signs by which the world, all corrupt though it be, recognises and admires love, and if love cannot always manifest itself by heroic sacrifices, it constantly shows by lesser immolations that it bears with it the germ which renders it as *strong as death*,[1] to use an expression of Solomon.

But devotedness is not possible without free will. To devote ourselves, we have said, is to prefer another to ourselves, is to give ourselves to another to be his own. Now, how can we give ourselves, if we are not free? How can we prefer another to ourselves, if we cannot dispose of ourselves? A being, deprived of free will, is under the fatal ascendancy of a foreign domination; he thinks, he moves only by the thought and will which hold him captive, by that inner captivity in which nothing remains to the proper action of his personality. Does such a being, thus despoiled of himself, preserve the right to give himself? He may die, but he dies as the stone falls, the slave of death and not of love. Even then, as free will is the condition of love, inasmuch as love is a sentiment of preference, it is also its condition, inasmuch as love is the impulsion of devotedness.

[1] Canticle of Canticles, viii. 6.

There remains a third act which crowns the marvellous drama of which our will is the theatre and the author. After we have chosen the object of our preference, after we have given ourselves to that object by sacrifice, all is not achieved. That object must prefer us, must give itself to us, and from that reciprocal choice and devotedness results a fusion of the two beings in the same thoughts, the same desires, the same wills—a fusion so ardent and so intimate that it would attain even to consummating them in one unique substance, if that power of joining substantial unity to personal plurality were not the exclusive privilege of the most holy and indivisible Trinity. At least we feel as it were the foreshadowing of this, and the limit where, with the power of union, the power of created love expires, is most painful to us. Union is the term of love, the term where it has nothing more to produce but the perseverance of its acts and the immortality of its happiness. But union, as well as preference and devotedness, needs free will; for to unite it is necessary to be two, and we are two only on condition of preserving on either part the plenitude of our personality, and this we cannot do without free will. The soul in which free will does not exist, or has never existed, which has never been capable of emitting a thought or an act of volition of its own, that soul is absorbed in another; it is annihilated by its powerlessness to be the equal of a free soul, and to give to it, in reciprocal love, the preference, devotedness, and union which it receives.

I know not if it be an illusion, but it seems to me that nothing is more clear than this essential relation between free will and love; and consequently nothing is more clear also than the reasons whence divine wisdom has drawn the resolution of placing us in the world with the perilous gift of liberty. God had no need of us; he has freely chosen to communicate his blessings to us and unite us to himself; he has also freely loved us. Now, in its nature, love exacts love; it is impossible to prefer without willing to be preferred, to devote ourselves without willing that our devotedness should be returned, and, as to union, it could hardly be conceived without the idea of reciprocity. Reciprocity is the law of love; it is the law of love between two equal beings; how much more so must it be between two beings of whom one is the creator and the other the creature; of whom one has given all, and the other has received all! God had an infinite right to be loved by man, because he had loved him with an eternal and infinite love, and consequently he should place man in the only condition in which he could render him preference for preference, devotedness for devotedness, union for union, that is to say, in the glory and trial of free will. It was the right of God; but, strange to say, it was also the right of man, or at least his honour, since, without that gift of free will, man would neither have been able to choose nor to devote himself, nor, consequently, to love in the true and generous sense of the word.

Ask, then, no longer why man is free; why he is not born in a state of perfection and beatitude without peril of failure. He is free, because he should love; he is free, because he should choose the object of his love; he is free, because he should devote himself to the object of his choice; he is free, because in the union which terminates love he should bring the stainless dowry of an entire personality; he is free, in fine, because God has freely loved him, and has willed to receive from him the equitable recompense of full reciprocity.

I do not, however, disguise to myself the difficulty which rises in your minds; it is grave, and I will endeavour to be its exact interpreter.

According to Catholic doctrine, the trial of free will ceases with the present life of man; once disappeared from this world and called before the supreme judge, man passes into a state of happy or miserable consummation which leaves him neither the honour, nor the danger, nor the resource of choice. If, then, free will be essential to the reality of love, it follows that the saints, in the beatitude of eternity, love God only under the form of incomplete and impersonal affection, which it is absurd to suppose.

Doubtless it is absurd to suppose, and I shall neither suppose nor say this. When the saints enter into heaven, vanquishers of death and life, they do not enter there deprived of their anterior existence, as beings without past, without future, without acquired habits; on the contrary, they enter into full possession of a personality laboriously perfected, with all their soul and all their works, according to that beautiful prophecy of the apostle St. John, who, by the Spirit of God, beholding the last days of the world, heard from on high a voice which said: *Blessed are the dead which die in the Lord . . . . for their works follow them.*[2] Their works follow them because they are living like them and in them, living in the love which was their fruit, and which mounts with the saints to heaven, not to lose there its primitive character of choice and devotedness, but to preserve it there for ever in the immutability of beatific vision. The saints have not another heart in heaven than that which they had on earth; the very object of their pilgrimage was to form in them, by means of trial, a

[2] Apocalypse xiv. 13.

love which should merit to please God and subsist eternally before him. So far from that love changing its nature, it is its nature itself, it is its degree acquired in the free exercise of the will which determines the measure of beatitude in each elect of grace and judgment. According as man brings to God more ardent affection, he derives deeper ecstacy, more perfect felicity from the vision of the divine essence. It is the movement of his heart, as death has seized it, which regulates his place at the seat of life, and it is the unalterable perseverance of that movement, caused by the view of God, which alone distinguishes the love of time from the love of eternity. God recognises in his saints the apostles, the martyrs, the virgins, the doctors, the hermits, the hospitallers, who have before confessed and served him in the tribulations of the world; the saints in their turn recognise in God the being to whom they gave their undivided love in the time of their suffering and their liberty. Nothing is foreign to them in the sentiments which they feel, nothing is new to them in their heart. They love him whom they had chosen; they enjoy him to whom they had given themselves; they ardently embrace him whom they already possessed; their love expands in the certainty and joy of an inamissible union; but it is not separated from the stalk that bore it. God gathers but does not detach it; he crowns but does not change it.

It is thus that the trial of free will ceases, and that, notwithstanding, love subsists entire in the soul where God rewards it. But up to this point there is a struggle in the heart of man between good and evil, between his tendency towards God by charity, and towards himself by the egotism of the passions. The outer world arms itself to overcome him by all the beauties which it has received in another design; it opposes the visible charm to the eternal order which should obtain all our regards and regulate all our acts. Balanced as we are between these two attractions, we need strength to keep us attached to the polar star of real good, and that strength we call by a still more illustrious name than that of love—we call it virtue. Love without virtue is but weakness and disorder; by virtue, it becomes the accomplishment of all duties, the bond that unites us first to God, next to all the creatures of God; it becomes justice and charity, two things which form but one, and which were given to us on the day of our creation, to be, after truth, the second means of responding to our destiny and attaining our end.

I should have nothing more to say to you if, now as always, we had not to seek in rationalism for the counterproof of the doctrine I have just exposed to you. This doctrine attests that there exists an infinite difference between good and evil, since good is God, inasmuch as he is order, and evil is opposition to order, that is to say, to God; it attests that good is the object of the will, its perfection, its beatitude, and that the will corresponds thereto by love, the disinterested fruit of free will and virtue; it affirms, in fine, that man, being free to love or to hate, to do or not to do good, is responsible for his actions before the supreme justice of God. Is this also the doctrine of rationalism? In affirming the contrary, I have no need to tell you that I take the word rationalism in its general acceptation, and not as representing this or that class of philosophers. Rationalism has but one principle, which is the sufficiency of reason alone to explain the mystery of destinies, but it has a thousand heads which contradict each other, and which consequently never bear together the responsibility of the same errors. This diversity discharges such philosopher from such condemnable system; it does not discharge rationalism, whose starting-point is the cause of all the dogmas that deceive thought by corrupting truth.

I wished to give you this explanation at the moment when rationalism is about to appear to you in its most odious form. Already you have seen it denying the existence of God, the creation of the world by God, the primitive intercourse between God and man, and placing in doubt even the very notion of truth. After such ruins, could it respect the distinction between good and evil? That distinction is but a consequence of the idea of God; this overthrown, the moral order disappears of itself. However, it is one thing to attack moral order in its source, another to attack it in front and directly. Were there nothing of God there, or were he a God indifferent to the acts of man, the soul might still endeavour to take refuge in itself, and by its own strength create for itself sacred duties. Notwithstanding the profundity of negations upon which it rests, it might choose not to deny itself, but by a generous contradiction, acknowledge laws and impose duties upon itself. However feeble that barrier may be, it is a vestige of conscience, an honour for man, a safeguard for society. What a crime, then, is it to dispute our possession of it, and pursue the idea of good even to the ruins amongst which we have formed this last and miserable refuge. Rationalism has not been ashamed to do this; after having attacked moral order in its principle, which is God, it has seized upon our soul as upon the remains of a prey, and defying us in this our supreme refuge, it contests the reality of love and the reality of free will.

Ingenuous that I was, I spoke to you but just now of sympathetic attractions, of disinterested preferences, of voluntary sacrifices. I represented to you the ascendancy of good over the heart of man; I deceived you, if we must believe rationalism, I deceived you cruelly, and myself with you. Would you know the truth? Man acts only from one single motive, his own interest; he calls good that which is useful to him, evil that which lessens the value of the things and enjoyments of which he is in possession. Duty, if he observe it, is but a means of preserving his rights; love, if he feel it, is but a sentiment of pleasure. Egotism is at the fount of every human act, under whatever appearance or whatever name it may be hidden; and those grand expressions of devotedness, abnegation, immolation of self, serve but to disguise our true inclinations under a show which flatters our pride. The mother loves and seeks herself in her child; the soldier idolises himself in the glory of his captain or his country; death even is atoned for by the admiration which causes us to live again, as we believe, in posterity. Assuredly, if we may hope to find in man a pure sentiment of personal interest, we should seek for it in the soul of the Christian, since Christianity reposes upon the mystery of a God who gratuitously died for us. And yet to what does the Christian devote his life? To labour for his salvation, that is to say, to avoid hell and obtain paradise. His most heroic works are but a bargain which he makes with God. He knows that they are all registered, that not one falls to the ground, and that he will one day find again the smallest particle in an increase of felicity. Is this forgetfulness of self? Is this that charity come down from heaven, immolated on a cross, and raised again from the tomb to live in the heart of generations? Alas! It would be better to confess our indelible egotism, and to recognise with the sincerity of true philosophy that every being, whatever it may be, acts and lives but for itself.

We are asked for an avowal; let us begin by making it. Yes, it is impossible for any being endowed with intelligence and will to separate himself completely from his acts. I think, I will, I love; in whatever way I may take it, it is I, myself, who thinks, who wills, who loves, and it is not in my power to take that I from myself. Whether I perform a good or a bad action, I am present in it, and have the enjoyment of it. Yet more, I should not perform it if I had no enjoyment in it. For every action supposes an end, and the last end of man being beatitude, for which

God has expressly created him, it is absolutely chimerical to imagine that he acts without having before him the thought and motive of his happiness. And let me ask you, was there no difference between Nero and Titus; between Nero killing his mother, and Titus contributing to the happiness of the human race? Is there no difference between the soldier who turns his back in a battle, and the soldier who dies with his face towards the enemy and his country in his heart? Leonidas at Thermopylæ, Demosthenes at Chæronea, are they the same? You may say so, but I defy you to think so. You will not even say so before an assembly of men who honour you by listening to your words; even if your conscience lie to itself, it would not be bold enough to lie in the face of mankind. If there is one individual here who confounds in the same estimation and the same contempt crime and virtue, let him stand up! let him speak! And yet it is most true: Titus, like Nero, sought his happiness; there was no difference between them on this head; and if egotism consists in willing to be happy, Titus was an egotist by the same title as Nero.

But does egotism consist in willing to be happy? This is precisely the question. It would be very strange if happiness and immorality should be one and the same thing. Happiness is the vocation of man; it is the natural and predestinate patrimony of all intelligent beings. Whoever among them comes into the world comes into it to be happy. It is his right: what do I say? It is his duty. For his duty is to obey God, and God has pointed out to him two equal and parallel orders in calling him into life; the order of perfection and the order of beatitude. But, remark attentively what I have said; happiness is the patrimony of all, of all without exception; it is the natal land and the future country of all those who have not voluntarily repudiated it. And from this a great consequence follows, it is that no one should attribute to himself the happiness of others, and that all being children of the same father, inheritors of the same kingdom, we are commanded to live together in the divine fraternity of one and the same beatitude. He who usurps the part of another, who would be happy at the expense of his brethren, who, by cunning or violence, divides the spotless and seamless garment of felicity, is guilty of a crime which includes all other crimes; he is guilty of egotism, and since the beginning of the world he has borne a name and a mark—the name of Cain, and the mark of reprobation. He, on the contrary, who desires to be happy with all, who takes from another no part of his patrimonial right to happiness, who gives even of his own, he also, since the beginning of the world, has borne a name and a mark—the name of Abel, and the mark of charity. Charity does not consist in being unhappy any more than egotism consists in being happy; it consists in not troubling the good of others, and in communicating to them our own; a communication which, so far from impoverishing, enriches at the same time the receiver and the giver. Good has received from God that admirable elasticity, that the sharing it multiplies without lessening it, and that falling from the right hand, it returns to the left, like the ocean which receives all the waters of the earth, because it renders them all back again to the heavens.

This explanation, you will say, justifies the intimate sentiment of mankind, which has always placed an infinite difference between good and evil, which has execrated Nero and idolised Titus; but, in granting that personal happiness is the necessary end of all the acts of man, do you not destroy the very notion of love and devotedness? How can there be any sacrifice, any preference of others to ourselves, where we seek ourselves?

I have not said that personal happiness was the necessary end of all the acts of man; for that word personal excludes from the happiness of each the happiness of all, and I have declared, on the contrary, that happiness is a universal and indivisible patrimony, which no one could appropriate exclusively to himself without being guilty of the crime of egotism. Learn, then, that duty, love, devotedness, consist in making of our happiness the happiness of others, and of the happiness of others our own happiness, whilst egotism consists in deriving happiness from the misfortunes of others. Nero wished the Roman people had but one head, that he might take it off at a single blow : this is egotism. Titus considered that day to be lost in which he failed to render some one happy : this is love. "To love," Leibnitz has said, "is to place our happiness in the happiness of another." That sublime definition needs no commentary: it is understood or not understood. He who has loved understands it ; he who has not loved will never understand it. He who has loved knows that a shadow in the heart of his choice would darken his own; he knows that nothing would be a sacrifice, prayers, tears, watchings, toil, privations, that would bring one smile upon the sorrowing lips ; he knows that he was dead to redeem a compromised life ; he knows that he was happy in another, happy in another's graces, happy in another's virtues, happy in another's glory, happy in that other's happiness, and that, had his blood been needed to increase that other's happiness, become his own, he would have given it, even to the last drop, with the sole regret of being able to die but once. He who has loved knows this. He who has not loved is ignorant of it; I pity him, and I do not reply to him.

I pity him, because he has known nothing either of human or of divine life; I do not reply to him, because the testimony of a dead man proves nothing against the living. What is it to us, Christians, if we must appeal to ourselves? what is it to be accused of indifference towards God by a man who has never loved God? Does he know what passes within us? Can he even conjecture it? He thinks that, with our eyes fixed upon heaven and hell, with our works in one hand, the scales in the other, we make a bargain with God for the price of our abnegation! He knows not that fear and hope are but the preliminaries of Christian initiation, and that in virtue of the first commandment, which includes all the others, according to the words even of Jesus Christ, the Christian ought to love God with all his heart, with all his mind, with all his strength, above all things, under the penalty, adds St. Paul, of *being nothing*.[3] He knows not that beyond the threshold of faith the soul is touched by the invisible beauty of

[3] 1 Corinthians xiii. 2.

a love which the most heroic affections of this world will never equal, either in endurance, depth, or sacrifice; and that that love drawing us into the abyss of charity where God himself respires, we draw therefrom the desire to associate all creatures in the perfection and felicity of which we have a foretaste, and of which we await the ulterior revelation. Who can deny this enlargement of the heart of man in Christianity? Who can deny it, save those who have never known what it is, and who, abased in the narrow passions of the senses, where all is egotism, measure by their own souls the soul of the Christian and the soul of man?

I am ashamed to prove to you the reality of love and devotedness, but rationalism compels me. It compels me also to say a few words to you on free will, which is, with disinterestedness, the principal condition of the moral order. As the moral order is destroyed if man acts only with a view to his interest, it is likewise destroyed if man be not master of his acts. Therefore, rationalism has not assailed our liberty with less ardour than our generosity; it needs our servitude as much as our egotism; our egotism to confound good with evil, our servitude to take from us the responsibility either of good or evil.

Are we free? Your conscience and mine answer:

Yes. Rationalism says: No. And does rationalism give any proof of this? None. It asks us, on the contrary, to prove that we are free, and if we oppose to it the testimony of our intimate conviction, which knows apparently what it judges, that is condemned as blind and insufficient. It fears that our intimate conviction may be the victim of a superior power, which, unknown to it, makes it the instrument of its irresistible will. For us who believe in God, who, bending the knee before his adorable supremacy, have acknowledged him as the father, the master, the principle, and the end of things, we do not entertain the strange doubts of rationalism in regard to what passes within us. Offspring of unequalled goodness and immeasurable wisdom, we do not imagine that God tortures his omnipotence to deceive the heart of his work, and give to it in servitude the illusion of liberty. We trust in the divine sincerity, and we do not seek whether it be in his power, even if he so willed, to lead us to so contradictory an impression on the subject of ourselves and our own acts. Truths, like errors, link together. God, once rejected or placed in doubt, I permit rationalism to mistrust the human conscience; the edifice being destroyed at its base, how can any detached part be sustained, and moreover, what interest would exist for so doing? What is man if God is not? What are good and evil? What the past and the future? It is needless for us to trouble ourselves about a dream in a night passed in sound sleep. But if God is, if the name that sustains all is written in the vault of our intelligence as in the vault of heaven, then I will no longer even listen to the rationalism which suggests mistrust to me on the subject of that liberty whose real presence I feel in myself. I take account of myself and of all things with me. My conscience is a sanctuary which gives me oracles; my life is a power which answers for itself; the divine solidity descends into all my being; and doubt, to my mind, is nothing but blasphemy and folly. I am free; I pass from good to evil, and from evil to good. Suspended between these two terms which infinity separates, a voluntary captive or a culpable rebel, at each moment I choose and decide my condition. I choose to love myself, or to love God above all things; I withdraw, I return, I obey, or I resist remorse; and even in crime, I feel my greatness by my sovereignty. I need but a tear to remount to heaven, but a look to fall back into the gulf. This struggle is great, this responsibility is terrible; but woe and scorn to him who descends from the throne from fear of the duties that sit there with him!

Must I, in concluding, enlighten that other difficulty which rationalism opposes to the reality of free will, and which it draws no longer from the vanity of our conscience, but from the very attributes of God? I will do so rapidly, fearing to weary your attention, and hoping to abuse it but little. Truth is brief, because it is clear.

Catholic doctrine ranges amongst the divine attributes, that of foreknowledge, that is to say, the anticipated and infallible knowledge of the future, even of the future which depends upon our free will. Now, how can God foresee this last kind of future, if it be not because he is master of our acts and directs them at pleasure? How does he know infallibly what I shall do to-morrow if not because he has decreed it, and because he possesses in his omnipotence the certainty of our determinations?

I shall have replied to this if I show, in the nature of God and in the nature of man, a means of foreseeing the effects of free causes which in no way destroys their liberty.

Now it is manifest that no reasonable being acts without motives, that is to say, without something that determines his actions. Hence these avowals constantly made by us: "Here is a reason, an interest, a circumstance, which decides me; in other terms, which persuades me to act." And when we examine the motives whose efficacious impression draws man from repose or uncertainty, we find that there are but two: the motives of duty and passion. Man decides either by a view of what is true, good, suitable; or by the inducement of a personal satisfaction independent of any idea of order. The question simply is to know who will decide him to the one or the other motive. If he were not free, the stronger attraction of his nature would decide him, as the greater weight brings down one of the scales of the balance. But man is free; between two attractions equal or unequal in themselves, it is he who pronounces sovereignly. Nevertheless he pronounces by virtue of a motive which persuades him, and not without cause, or arbitrarily. He knows what he does and why he acts; he knows even why he is persuaded to act. Persuasion reaches him not only from without, it comes to him especially from within, from the intimate state of his will, from his tastes, his virtues—the fruit of free will, free will itself in activity, such as it is formed, such as it wills to be, such as it presents itself to the outer attractions which come to solicit him for good and evil. It is the state of volition, the seat of free will, that decides the choice of man between the two motives of duty and passion.

Suppose that state known, you would know what man would do in a given case, and in all the cases where the knowledge of the soul would for you have preceded its actions. Such is the basis of human, as well as of divine, knowledge. Have you never confided your fortune or your honour to the word of a man? You have done so; or, if you have never had occasion, you name within yourselves those to whom you would voluntarily give a high mark of your esteem. Whence comes that assurance? How are you certain that you will not expose your life to treason? You are sure of it, because you know the soul to whom you abandon your own; that knowledge is sufficient for you to see that in no case, under whatever peril or temptation, will your fortune or your honour be basely sacrificed.

They may be, however; the heart to which you give your faith is fallible, it is subject to unforeseen assaults; it matters not, you sleep peacefully, and no one accuses you of imprudence or credulity. If it happen that you are deceived, what will you say? You will say, "I was mistaken in that man, I thought him incapable of a bad action." Such is the chance which you would run, the chance of being mistaken; because, being a finite intelligence, you cannot read directly in the soul of another, nor even in the depths of your own. Whence it results that you possess only a moral certainty of your judgments, and of your foresight only an assurance of the same degree.

It is not the same with God. *God*, to use the expression of Saint Paul, *penetrates even to the division of the soul and the spirit, of the joints also and the marrow of our being, and is a discerner of the thoughts and intents of the heart.*[4] We are eternally naked before him. He sees with infinite precision the state of our will, and, knowing in the same light all the outward circumstances to which we are exposed, he possesses an infallible certainty of the choice we shall make between good and evil, between the motives of duty and passion. From that moment, he knows our history, which is but a struggle more or less prolonged between the two opposite attractions, one which bears us towards our real end, another which turns us aside towards a base or false end. And that anticipated knowledge of ourselves being in no way the cause of our acts, no more obstructs our liberty than if it did not exist.

The error in this matter is in supposing free will to be a kind of abstract power, independent in its proper state, having no other movement than unlimited caprice. If it were so, man himself would

[4] Hebrews iv. 12.

not be capable of foreseeing his own actions an instant beforehand. His sovereignty would be but a state of permanent unreason. He would choose between good and evil without knowing why, and passing at hazard from crime to virtue, because of his liberty, we should find in him nothing more than an unregulated automaton. Such is neither man nor free will; I have shown you this, and I have but to leave your conscience to choose between the ethics of Christianity and the ethics of rationalism.

Christianity leads to charity and liberty; rationalism to egotism and fatality. If in the preceding questions, which appeal only to reason, some slight cloud still obscured your need of light, that cloud has vanished. The abyss of error has enlightened the abyss of truth. As the speculative dogmas of the existence of God, the Trinity, creation, the substantial diversity of matter and spirit, the vocation of man to perfection and beatitude, lead to the practical dogma of the distinction of good and evil; so the speculative dogmas of pantheism, dualism, materialism, scepticism, lead to the practical dogma of the confusion of good and evil, the supreme term which discerns all, and where darkness becomes light.

MAN AS A SOCIAL BEING.

My Lord,—Gentlemen,

WHEN God had made man, and when, after having animated him with the breath of life, he also shed in his soul light and justice—the light of truth and the justice of charity, he halted, if I may so speak, to contemplate his work, and seeing the eyes of man opening, his ears hearing, his lips trembling with the first vibration of speech, that clay, in fine, which he had touched with his mighty hand, become a sensible and a reasonable creature, he remained thoughtful, as if something were wanting to the masterpiece he had just produced. In fact, the mystery of our creation was not accomplished; God withdrew a second time within himself to stamp our nature with the seal of a higher perfection, and beforehand he declared his design by saying : " Non

EST BONUM ESSE HOMINUM SOLUM." *It is not good for man to be alone.*[1]

Why was it not good for man to be alone? In what manner was he to cease to be alone? This is the object which I now propose to your meditations, and in which you will see that society is the third primitive gift with which God has endowed us, the third means given to help us in the fulfilment of our destiny.

No being is alone. Whether we look above or below us, in God or in nature, we see plurality and association on every hand. God, who is one, is not solitary; he includes three persons in the unity of his substance, and the inferior world, divided into an innumerable multitude of different groups, presents none of which the condition and law of the creature is solitude. At each degree of existence we find number and union, that is to say society. Number without union would still be only isolation; but when beings, distinct by individuality, alike by nature, approach and give each other their life, blend together reciprocally, act upon each other by mutual relations, then there is society, and such is the state of all creatures inferior to man; such is the state, under a more perfect mode, of the divine persons in

[1] Genesis ii. 18.

heaven. Endeavour to imagine an absolutely solitary being, that is to say a being who has no resemblance or relations to anything, you will but create an abstract phantom in your imagination, a sort of God—nothing, because it would be at the same time infinite and void, infinite from want of bounds, void from want of activity. Isolation is the negation of life, since life is a spontaneous movement, and since movement supposes relations; still much more is it the negation of order, harmony, and beauty, all perfection and all beatitude, since none of those things can be conceived without the double idea of plurality and unity. Plurality without unity is positive disorder; unity without plurality is negative disorder. In the first case, the bond is wanting to the beings; in the second, the beings are wanting to the bond. Now, wherever there is disorder, it is evident that harmony, beauty, perfection, and beatitude vanish at the same time. It was then with justice that God, regarding man in the solitude of his creation, pronounced the words: *It is not good for man to be alone.*

It is true that, by his intermediary position between the superior and inferior worlds, man—body and spirit—found himself in relation with nature and God; but that double relation did not the less leave him alone of his species, alone in the rank he occupied, a sort of stylite lost between earth and heaven. Even had nature sufficed for the wants of his body and God for the wants of his spirit, man, deprived of relations with beings of the same form and degree, would not have sufficed for the greatness of the position which he was charged to occupy. His history would have been too short, his perils too limited, his virtues too restrained; as he had a world above and below himself, it was needful that he should become a world, and that in this manner all the parts of creation, although unequal in themselves by their place and their essence, should answer to each other in a certain proportion of immensity. Man was to extend without being divided, to increase in number in order to increase in union, and to become, in the majesty of number and the harmony of union, a theatre of virtues such as the perfection of the universe and his own perfection required. Circumscribed in isolation, God alone would have been the object of his duties; member of a body composed of beings like himself, his offices embrace, with God, the whole of mankind. The law of love, the sum of all justice, no longer radiated only from the creature to the creator; it animated with its life all the orbs of creation.

This great work is before your eyes; for sixty centuries human society has covered the field of history with its institutions. Stronger than time, it has resisted all disasters, and has constantly recovered its youth in the ruins under which degenerate nations have buried themselves. It is human society which has led our infancy through the hazards of the primitive emigrations, which divided the earth for us, and, after having dispersed us upon all the habitable shores, drew us together in spite of the jealousy of the deserts and the tempests of the ocean. It is human society which has built celebrated cities, encouraged arts, founded sciences, propagated letters, raised the mind of man to perfection, and given to his heart the glory of all virtues with the occasion of all sacrifices. In fine, human society is the permanent mode of our terrestrial life; and if, in the depths of forests or on the rocky shores of distant isles, the traveller discovers groups of people deprived of all civilization, he still finds among them some rudiments of the social state, certain vestiges or outlines of relations which show how incapable man is to live alone.

And yet, who would believe it? the dogma of society has not been subject to fewer attacks than the rest. As sages have been found to deny God, creation, the distinction of matter and spirit, truth, the difference between good and evil, there have also been found men who maintain that society is a purely human institution, and, yet much more, that it is an institution against nature. They have endeavoured to persuade us that society is the source of all our evils, and that with our civilization our decadency began. Who among us, in the time of his youth, has not imagined himself wandering freely in the solitudes of the new world, having no roof but the heavens, no drink but the water of unknown streams, no food but the spontaneous fruit of the earth and the game which fell by his hand, no law but his will, no pleasure but the continual feeling of his independence and the chances of a life without limits on a soil without possessors? These were our dreams. Our heart, recognising itself, thrilled when our eyes fell upon that passage in a celebrated book, where the man of civilization says to the man of the desert: " Chactas, return into thy forests; take up again that holy independence of nature which Lopez will no longer deprive thee of; were I younger, I would follow thee." On reading these words it seemed that we heard them ourselves; our oppressed soul soared with them into ideal regions, and returned but with pain to the monotonous burden of reality.

Were we then in the true ? Was that movement of our soul out of society an aspiration towards the primitive state which God had made for us, or a revolt against the order established by Providence in our favour? It was a revolt, a bound of egotism impatient of the limits which universal communion with our fellow-creatures imposes upon us, an attempt to subject the universe to our individuality alone. Whilst, in the plan of divine goodness, happiness is the right and patrimony of all, we sought to leave mankind in order to withdraw from sharing its blessings and evils, and rid ourselves of the duties which inevitably result from a great assemblage of relations. We hate dependence and labour in society. Dependence first : for society exists only by unity; unity is formed by ties; those ties, when intelligent beings are concerned, change into obligatory laws for the conscience, and are maintained by the double authority of public power and opinion. This is a yoke accepted by the virtue which does not separate its condition from the condition of others, but which weighs upon the egotism that lives only for itself; and therefore, as solitude is destructive of all laws because it destroys all relations, egotism seeks solitude in order to escape from dependence. In no less a degree it hates labour, another consequence of civilization. A few men scattered over an immense territory live at little cost. Nature, abandoned to herself, supplies their wants, and isolation lessening in them the attraction which reproduces life, their number increases so slowly that it does not disturb their indolence. The man of society, on the contrary, has a paternity as prolific as his heart; he sees, under the blessing of God, the family changing into a tribe, the tribe into a community, the community into a nation; the tents are sheltered under walls; territories are defined by boundaries; nature fails before the increase of mankind. Art must supply its want of space and vigour. Assiduous labour must second the inventions of art. Numberless employments solicit the arms of men, and the arms of men in their turn solicit employment. Our veins are filled with the fruit of our toil. Each drop of our blood is purchased from the land at the price of a virtue.

This is more than enough to alarm egotism, and persuade it that social order is but an imposture in a state of martyrdom. I do not refute it, I simply explain to you how it is that the Christian dogma of society has contradictors and enemies. Dependence, labour, are hard words, I cannot deny it; and whoever does not accept them is necessarily in revolt against the reality of human things.

But a few days ago, you engraved upon the monuments of your capital that memorable inscription : *Liberty, equality, fraternity.* It is, in fact, a part of the primitive charter which has united men together and founded the human race ; but it is not the whole of it. It is the charter of rights, not that of duties. Now man, living in society, can no more deprive himself of duties than of rights. If liberty is necessary, that he may remain a moral creature, that he may not be overwhelmed in the pressure of an exaggerated and unjust domination, obedience is also necessary, to enable him to keep his place, by the help of a common and sacred law, in the living home which a nation makes for him. If equality is necessary, that he may not decline from the rank in which God has placed him by a common origin with all his fellow-creatures, hierarchy is also necessary that he may not, in default of a chief and a commanding authority, fall into the powerlessness of individual dissolution. If fraternity is necessary in order that confidence and love might widen the narrow ties of social order, that mankind might remain one great family sprung from one common father, veneration is also necessary, to acknowledge and strengthen the authority of age, the magistracy of virtue, the power of laws, in those who possess this character whether as legislators or as sovereigns. Write then, if you would found durable institutions, write above the word liberty, obedience; above equality, hierarchy; above fraternity, veneration; above the august symbol of rights, the divine symbol of duties. I have said this to you elsewhere; right, is the selfish side of justice; duty, is its generous and devoted side. Appeal from it to devotedness, that devotedness may respond to you, and that your work may triumph over the ardent passions, which, since the origin of society, have never ceased to conspire for its ruin.

Human society is not only hated for itself, on account of the duties that it imposes, it is also hated for another reason which it is important for you to learn. God, who was the founder of society, is its preserver. He maintains it by the power of his name, which is perpetuated under the guardianship of dogmatic traditions and religious observances. No nation has been able to exist without that venerated name, no community has been built up without that corner-stone of the temple. And vainly will the impious hope to abolish the memory of God until that society be abolished which is its depository, and which lives upon this hereditary treasure of mankind.

Human society and religious society are two sisters born on the same day of the divine word, the one having regard to time, the other to eternity; distinct in their domain and end, but indissolubly united in the heart of man, sustaining one another, falling together, rising again together, braving together by their common immortality the hatred that pursues both of them. Do not lose this point of view, if you would take account of the leaven of anarchy which rouses the heart of man against society. Society is no other thing than order, and order has in God its invulnerable root. Whoever does not love God has by that alone a permanent cause of aversion towards the social state, which could not do without God.

Thence it comes that anti-religious epochs infallibly produce anti-social theories. You witnessed this in the last century. Whilst the doctors of a superficial generation held up to ridicule Jesus Christ, the Bible, and the Church, others, with a pen no less bold, wrote against human society. The savage state was exalted as the primitive state of man, and incomparably the best; the effeminate gentlemen of the Trianon were invited to return to that state with bows and arrows in their hands. It was demonstrated that society was at least formed by a voluntary contract,

Man as a Social Being.

and, with a gravity but too formidable, they sought the clauses of that fabulous contract.'

Is it necessary for me to prove to you that social order is neither an institution against nature, nor a facultative institution? We are far removed from the time when men discussed these questions, puerile in themselves, but which were rendered important by the decadency of the monarchy under which they were treated. Now that this monarchy has disappeared in a tempest, and the epoch of reconstruction has succeeded to that of ruins, intelligent minds are interested much more about the economical problems of social life than about the circumstances of its origin and the primary causes of its establishment. Therefore I shall confine myself to the few words which are necessary rationally to confirm the dogma of society such as Catholic doctrine professes it.

A thing is natural when it is in conformity with the real constitution of a being. Now the social state is evidently in conformity with the constitution of man, since everywhere and always he has lived in society. It is true that some oppose to us the savage tribes of America, and of many islands scattered in the ocean; but those very tribes, although deprived of civilization, live nevertheless in the unformed rudiments of community. They are branches accidentally detached from the great human trunk, and which, deprived of the sap of traditions, withdrawn from the law of oral instruction, vegetate on the extreme confines of sociability without having burst the last link that holds them thereto. If truth and charity should seek them at the ends of the world; if the words of the gospel, borne by the clouds of heaven, should fall upon the uncultivated glebe of their souls, you will see them extending their hands to the apostolate, covering their nakedness, plunging the plough into their forests, assembling round the wood and sign of a cross, and bowing their heads before the invisible presence of God, of whom they know nothing save a remembrance as uncertain as their life. You are not ignorant that Oceania now witnesses the accomplishment of these marvels, and those fortunate islands send back even to our old continents the virginal balm of a civilization which finds again a cradle in the ruins of the desert.

I do not mean to say that the savage passes easily, or that he always advances, to the state of social perfection; no, gentlemen, this is a difficult work which requires time, a combination of favourable circumstances, and which, on this account, is rarely crowned with success. An entire population is not drawn in a single day out of the torpor of an inveterate state of indolence and free indulgence of the passions. It is enough that it has been done, or even that it has been begun, for the savage state to cease to be an objection against the social temperament of man. The Iroquois, or the Huron, is not civilised, but he is fit for civilisation, and if he does not become civilised alone, by the aid of his proper forces, it is for the same reason that the deaf are dumb. No one is an initiator to himself; every man or every tribe having left society, which is the great and universal initiator, can return to it only by means of a legislator bringing from the common centre, truth, justice, order, and devotedness. We need not travel to the Pacific Ocean to find the savage; whoever rejects the social tradition, by ungoverned passions, is a voluntary savage; so much the more degraded as he touches the source of truth and goodness. You have met with those beings fallen by their fault below civilisation, and assuredly you have drawn no conclusions from their moral misery against the dignity of our nature and against its sociability. The exception has never destroyed a rule, and here there is not even an exception. The savage is to the civilised man what an abortion is to a plant which has received a regular development; by its very deformity it bears witness in favour of the normal type to the plenitude of which it has not attained.

Man lives then socially by virtue of his native constitution; he is naturally sociable, and consequently naturally social. It is not a facultative contract which has placed him in society; he is born in society. And if it happen that he leaves it by a lamentable accident which separates him from the common stock, it is impossible for him to return to it of himself under the form of a contract or a deliberation. He vegetates in that state until the civilised man touches his hand, and raises him by the fraternal sovereignty of language to the rank of an intelligent being enlightened by God. For it is God who first initiated the human race to the social life, and who, after having with truth and love deposited in mankind the germ of mutual attraction, gave to it the first impulsion. Truth and love are the basis of social order; wherever souls meet, having received these gifts, the principle of society meets in, and tends to unite, them. But this principle may be deadened or degraded, and this is why it exacts, all pre-existing though it may be, an initiatory intervention, to rouse it if it be deadened, to purify it if it be degraded. So that these two things are equally true, namely, that society is natural to man, and that it is nevertheless of divine institution. It is natural to man; because man, an intelligent and a moral being, has received in his creation the intelligible germ of truth and love: it is of divine institution; because it is God who first placed man in active possession of truth and love, and who, the first also, gave him the opportunity of applying truth and love in relations of like to like, of equal to equal.

It is time for us to arrive at that supreme moment of the drama of creation, and see human society unfolding under the blessed hand to whom we owe all.

When God had uttered that beautiful expression: *It is not good for man to be alone*, the Scriptures tell us that he caused a deep and mysterious sleep to fall upon Adam, our first father. It would seem that God, so to say, feared to be troubled by the look of man during the sublime work he was about to perform; he willed that no other thought than his own should intervene in the act which was about to give plurality to man without destroying his unity. For such was the work which his sovereign power purposed to accomplish. Taking the eternal order of the divine society as the pattern of human society, he designed that there should not only be moral unity in the relations between man and man ; but that those relations should take their source in one substantial unity, imitating as much as possible the tie that unites the three uncreated persons in an ineffable perfection. Mankind was to be one by nature, by origin, by blood ; and, by means of that triple unity, to form but one single soul and one single body of all its members. This plan was in conformity with the general end of God, which was to create us in his image and after his likeness, in order to communicate to us all his blessings ; it was worthy of his wisdom as well as of his goodness, and when I think that vulgar impiety has been able to laugh at the magnificent act which realised it, I am overwhelmed with pity for the abasement to which the intelligence falls that misunderstands the intelligence of God.

Man was, then, at the feet of his creator and father, overcome by the inertness of a superhuman sleep, knowing nothing of what was intended for him, and God looked thoughtfully upon him. Was it necessary to divide that beautiful creature in order to multiply him ? Was it necessary to create by his side an image of himself, without other community than likeness, and cause the human race to spring from one primitive being associated with a second ? It would have destroyed unity in the very root from whence it should blossom. There would have been two bloods, and only one was required. It was needful that all mankind should come from one single man, in order that living plurality should spring from living unity, and that man, multiplied without division, should recognise in his fellow creature, emanated from himself, *the bone of his bones and the flesh of his flesh.*[2] With this thought God bends towards man and is about to touch him: but where will he touch him? The brow of man, where with his intelligence reposes the eminent seat of his beauty, naturally presents itself to the creating hand, and seems to invite the new benediction about to descend upon us. God did not touch it. However beautiful the faculty of intelligence may be, it is not the term of our perfection. Calm as light, and cold also, it was not from the point which corresponds to him in the outer architecture of man that God was to draw forth the miracle of our consubstantial plurality. He knew a better part, he placed his hand upon it. He placed it upon the bosom of man; there, where the heart by its movement marks the course of life; there, where all the holy affections have their echo and rebound. God listened for a

[2] Genesis ii. 23.

moment to that heart so pure which he had just created, and by a thought of his omnipotence removing a part of the natural shield that covered it, he formed woman of the flesh of man, and her soul of the same breath which had made the soul of Adam.

Man saw his fellow-creature. He saw himself in another with his majesty, his strength, his gentleness; and with an additional grace, a delicate tint that manifested a dissemblance only to produce a more perfect fusion between the two parts of himself. First regard of man upon his fellow-creature, what was it? First nuptial moment of mankind, who shall reveal it? We will not endeavour to paint it, we will not lessen by vain poesy the solemnity of that wedlock whose consecrator was God; but imitating the austere simplicity of Scripture, we will repeat what it says to us.

After, then, God had led to man his companion, according to the expression of the sacred pages, he pronounced over them in these terms the blessing of inexhaustible fecundity: *Increase and multiply, and fill the earth.*[3] And with these words, efficacious like all the words of God, man received the gift of producing and perpetuating the miracle of the

[3] Genesis i. 28.

diffusion of his being, in offshoots personally distinct from himself, but one with him in form and blood. Mankind was founded, and the man in whom it had just become being, the man king, husband, father, bearing in himself the innumerable posterity of his sons, sang the hymn of the first nuptials, the song of the first love, the law of the first family, the prophecy of all generations. Listen, gentlemen, listen to our forefather speaking to his race in the name of God; listen to those first words of man which have traversed ages and taught the human race. *This*, said he, *is bone of my bones, and flesh of my flesh; she shall be called woman, because she was taken out of man; wherefore shall a man leave father and mother, and shall cleave to his wife; and they shall be two in one flesh.*[4] Such is the law of family, society, civilisation; such is the oracle which will for ever regulate the condition of mankind. Every legislator who may despise its commandment will but found barbarism; no nation that withdraws from it will ever attain to the era of justice and holy morality. It is upon the constitution of family that the progress or decadency of society will in all ages depend; and the constitution of family, signed by man and God, is written in the charter which has

[4] Genesis ii. 23, 24.

just been proclaimed to you. Woman is not to be the slave of man; she must be his sister, bone of his bones, flesh of his flesh. Wherever she may be degraded from this rank, man himself will be degraded; he will never know the pure joys of true love. Subjected to the domination of the senses, woman would be nothing to him but an instrument of sensuality; she would not speak to him of God with the authority of tenderness; she would not soften his heart by the constant charm of her own; she would not adorn his life by the innate delicacy of her voice and gesture. The domestic threshold, as the symbol of servitude, instead of recalling to man the holy and happy hours of his terrestrial passage, would recall to him only the inconstancy of his pleasures, the tyranny of his passions.

But woman is not only to be the sister of man by virtue of community of origin, she is to be his wife; in the virginity of her body and her soul she is to bring to him an inestimable gift, a gift which man will not be able to receive from another until death shall have broken the oath which purchased it. *She shall be called woman*, said Adam; *therefore a man shall leave his father and mother, and shall cleave unto his wife; and they shall be two in one flesh.* They shall be two, and not more than two;

they shall be two even to being but one flesh; and as death dissolves the unity of the flesh, death alone also shall destroy the unity of marriage, the source of life. Should the frailty of the human heart forget that order, should it profane marriage by daring to elevate adultery to the sanctity of marriage, woman would no longer exist either as wife or as mother. The infant born of her by an imperfect union would recognise in her only a dishonoured victim, and in his own days nothing but the fruit of selfish paternity.

Therefore, fraternal alliance between man and woman, exclusive and indissoluble alliance, in which, however, man exercises the chief authority, because he is the trunk whence his companion was taken, and because she was given to him by God, according to the language of Scripture, as *a help like unto himself*.[5] Such is the regular constitution of family, without which there is but oppression of the woman and child, weakening of the sense of moral obligation, sensuality instead of love, selfishness instead of devotedness, and in fine, barbarism or decadency, according to the age of the nations which have been led to despise the fundamental laws of society. Society is but the development of family; if man

[5] Genesis ii. 18.

leave his family corrupted, he will enter corrupted into the community. If the community would destroy family in order to regenerate itself, it would substitute an order factitious and against nature for the order established by God, and fall into the double abyss of unmeasured tyranny and licentious dissolution. It would be the high road to death.

Society being but the development of family, the general laws that regulate family regulate society also. As at the domestic hearth woman is the sister of man, the citizen at the forum is the brother of his fellow citizen; as man is only the husband of one wife, the citizen belongs only to one nation; as, in fine, the wife and child owe obedience and respect to the father, the citizen owes obedience and respect to the magistrate. If from the community we survey the human race, we shall recognise there, notwithstanding the difference of language, customs, and physiognomy, the dispersed council of a single race, the branching out of a single stem, and shall say to each man: Thou art my brother; to each nation: Thou art my sister; to all, whatever may be their colour, their history, or their name: This is bone of my bones, and flesh of my flesh. It is true we shall no longer find in the human race the unity of one single father, common obedience, unanimous respect; that order has been destroyed. The fields of Babylon saw the branches of man breaking off with great noise, and heard our forefathers utter in confused language the adieu of a separation which still exists. But the hour of the unity prepared and begun by Christ seems to draw near; the mountains bend, the seas diminish, the Christian family, with the vicar of God at its head, urges on, and, by its superiority henceforth assumed, enlightens the nations which have not yet adored the regenerating language of the gospel. The desire for peace keeps the sword in its sheath; fraternal language is exchanged from one end of the world to the other; the negro sits down with the white man in the great assemblies of nations; everything forebodes to attentive minds an era of reconciliation and the age in which, without destroying the variety or liberty of nations, the antique prophecy will be accomplished which announces to us, *one single shepherd for one single fold.*[6]

I halt before this glorious hope which should console all who are concerned about the future of the human race. How is it that here also I find rationalism as the adversary of the truths which so

[6] St. John x. 16.

greatly interest the dignity and happiness of man? Not content with having presented the social state as a state against nature, rationalism has attacked its constitution under three important relations: it has denied the unity of the human race, the unity of marriage, and its indissolubility. I shall not notice the two last errors, having had occasion to touch upon them in the Conference in which we treated *of the influence of Catholic society upon natural society in regard to family*, and I shall limit myself to confirming, in a few words, the substantial unity which makes of the human race a family issued from a single love, and from one and the same blood.

It seems that in the age we live in, an age wherein ideas of equality and fraternity generally predominate, if there is a dogma which should escape from negation, it is the dogma that gathers into unity all the nations that form mankind. But rationalism thought to seize Christian truth here in the very fact against the documents of science, and could not lose the opportunity of compromising it in those minds which attach more weight to the appearance of things than to the evidence of their laws. It endeavours then to establish the absolute diversity of the human races by the comparative study of the profound dissimilarities that mark their most important branches. These dissimilarities cannot be denied; the ignorant discover them as well as the learned. The Malay, the Mongol, the negro, have characteristic features which do not permit us to confound them either among themselves or with the European. This is true. The whole question is whether the difference is substantial, or only an accident, whether it constitutes a separate nature having an origin of its own; or whether it is but a shade caused in a primitive uniform type by the circumstances of time, place, customs, and even by fortuitous events whose effect and impress are afterwards perpetuated.

It is incontestable that sensible varieties appear in beings of the same kind and of the same progeny; it is the result of two forces which keep life in a just equilibrium, namely: spontaniety and immutability. Without spontaniety, that is to say, without a proper and original movement, beings would remain in the monotonous mould of barren uniformity; without immutability, they would lose the type of their true organisation under the force of their individual action. They are, then, at the same time free and restrained; they become modified without losing their nature. Such is the cause of those changes of physiognomy which have no name when they are not perpetuated; and which are called varieties when they are powerful enough to be transmitted and maintained. For, as the primitive form of the living being resists all mutations, the secondary or acquired form may also share this privilege when the causes that produced it are inveterate, and have passed, so to say, to the very roots of life. The father or mother, and sometimes both together, communicate to their children the features and expression which they themselves received from their authors. If this hereditary vestige promptly disappears in families of little distinction, it acquires an obstinate persistence in the more strongly marked races, which guard their blood with more watchful care. It is above all remarkable in the particular physiognomy of each nation, whatever approximation of climate or customs may exist between them. The Frenchman, the Englishman, the German, the Italian, the Spaniard, who touch each other on a soil limited in extent, who drink the same waters, and are invigorated by the same sun, who adore the same God, who have been mingled by an uninterrupted communion of from twelve to fourteen centuries, have a type of face personal to each, and by which they are instantly recognised by the least attentive observer. If it be so among nations subject to the influence of common elements, what must it be of those separated by distance, light, heat, food, religion, customs, all those material and spiritual causes, in fine, which act upon life and produce profound modifications? And if the dissimilarity of two European nations does not manifest the diversity of their primitive origin, how should the dissimilarity between the negro and the white man manifest anything but the diversity of their religious, political, and natural history? That which makes man is an intelligent soul united to a body endowed with certain proportions. Now has not the negro the same soul as the white man, and has he not the same body? Who will say that the soul of the negro is not human, and that his body is not human? And if the soul of the negro be human, if his body be human, is he not a man? And if he be a man, why should he not have had the same father as yourselves?

A physiological law, promulgated by the illustrious Cuvier, has also decided the question. It is known to science that all living beings which unite together, and whose posterity remains indefinitely prolific, belong to the same nature and remount to a primordially unique stem. In order to maintain the great lines of creation God has not willed that beings of diverse origin and kind should be able, by means of capricious alliances, to confound all bloods. Should this irregular event happen it may obtain from deceived fecundity a first result; but it never advances beyond this; order immediately reassumes its empire, and sterility punishes the fruit of a connection reproved by the will of the Creator. Now this anathema does not reach the union of the negro and the white man; their oaths received at the feet of the same altars, under the invocation of the same God, obtain in an indefinite posterity the glory of an act legitimate and holy. Much more, the two bloods recognise each other; the purer elevates to its splendour the one which had contracted an adulteration; from degree to degree, from alliance to alliance, all disparity vanishes, and the sons of Adam find themselves again, as sixty centuries ago, in the fraternal features of their common father.

Away, then, with those shameful attempts of fratricidal science. Let us no longer listen to the voices which do not respect the inviolable unity of the human race! Rather, Christians, let us hail from afar, and on every hand, let us hail our brethren dispersed by the tempest on such diverse shores. Let us, who have better preserved the primitive tint of our creation, who have received with a softer influence of natural light a better share of uncreated light; let us, the elder sons of truth and civilisation, hail our brethren whom we have preceded only to lead, whom we have surpassed only that they may one day equal us. Let us hail in them our past and our future unity, the unity which they had in Adam and that which we wait for in God. Let us stretch out our hands to the Malay and the Mongol; to the negro, the poor and the leper. All together, uniting our blessings and our misfortunes in one immense and sincere act of brotherhood, let us draw near to God, our first father. Let us draw near to God who made us from the same clay, who vivified us with the same breath, who has penetrated us with the same spirit, who has given us the same word, who has said to all of us: *Increase and multiply, and fill the earth, and subdue it, and rule over it.* He alone can bless us; he alone can open to us a veritable era of liberty, equality, and fraternity. Without him you will write those sublime words in vain upon your public monuments. Thirty centuries ago, they were written on the tables of Sinai by a more powerful hand than yours, and yet the tables of Sinai fell from the hands that carried them, and were broken in pieces at the foot of the mountain. It was because their laws were written in stone, and not in the heart of man. Write not then yours upon stone, write them with the finger of God in your own hearts, that they may speak therefrom to the hearts of all, and so ensure a durable immortality.

THE DOUBLE WORK OF MAN.

My Lord,—Gentlemen,

It remained for me to treat of the condition in which God created man as a physical being, and afterwards as a religious being. Under the first head, God endowed him with immortality; under the second, he prepared him for sharing the divine life itself by a gift which Catholic doctrine calls grace, that is to say, the gift *par excellence*. This should then be the present object of your attention. But having at a future period to treat before you of the mystery of the resurrection of the body, I reserve for that period all that concerns the exterior immortality of man ; and as to his vocation to sharing the divine life by the effusion of grace, it is too vast a subject to be dealt with on the day which will close our Conferences for this year. I reserve it also, then, and I am consequently led to the expression which in the Scriptures closes the account of creation. That expression is singular; it is as follows: *On the seventh day God ended his work which he had made; and he rested on the seventh day from all his work which he had done: and he blessed the seventh day, and sanctified it: because in it he had rested from all his work which God created and made.*[1]

By this you see that the world was not the work of a moment, but that God produced it in a progressive order distributed in six epochs, which the Scriptures call days. I shall not stop to expose or to justify that order, which is already known to you, Science has taken this upon itself during half a century; each of its discoveries comes unawares to prove the profundity of biblical cosmogony, and at length the bowels of the earth, brought to light by tardy investigations, have revealed, in the state of their different strata, the reality of the successive formation which is the basis of the account in Genesis. It was necessary to acknowledge either that Moses was inspired by God, or that, fifteen centuries before the Christian era, he possessed a science which was not to be disclosed until three thousand years later. I would willingly treat of this magnificent triumph of our faith, if the

[1] Genesis ii. 2, 3.

nature of my labours permitted me to add thereto the weight of a personal authority, and if it were not more fitting that whatever concerns scientific developments should rather be treated in a book than from a Christian pulpit. I confine myself then to this incontestable fact, that the Christian cosmogony is henceforth assured of the respect of all who do not despise the testimony of the most authentic realities. But this testimony, which suffices to confound the reproaches of the mind, does not suffice to satisfy its desire to know. It still asks why God created the world gradually, why he in a manner diminished his power to restrain his action. It is easy to conceive that time may be necessary to a finite cause; it is not easy to conceive its utility to a cause which can do all things of itself. How is it that God abased himself to the measure of a common workman? How is it that he began, quitted, and returned to his work? How is it that he rested from it? All these ideas are strange, and in seeing them united to the first act which has revealed God to us, to the act of creation, the intelligence vacillates and remains under the weight of unappeasable wonder.

I dare to say that your instinct deceives you, and that there is nothing greater in God than his abasement. Yes, God abased himself in creation, as we shall see him at a later period abasing himself in the incarnation and in the redemption; he abased himself because he laboured for us and not for himself, because strength and greatness are communicated only by descending. Yes, God had no need of time as an auxiliary to his eternity: no motive drawn from himself induced him to divide the formation of the earth into six periods, and to await the help of ages for that which depended upon an act of his sovereign thought. But if it were the same for him to act suddenly or slowly, it was not so for man. Destined, in our passage upon earth, to a work which ends only with itself and us, it is important for us to know the general law of labour; and God, in establishing outside of himself the operation whence all ulterior operation was to flow, willed that his manner of proceeding should for ever contain and reveal the rule of our own activity. That rule indeed has never been effaced from the memory of the human race. It has outlived the wreck of the most sacred traditions, and its vestiges are found in the division of time observed by most of the ancient and modern nations. But in order to comprehend in what it consisted, what was its object and its importance, it is necessary to take account of the labour even of man.

This word labour seems to awaken an idea incompatible with the primitive state in which God placed us; a state of perfection and happiness which I have represented to you, and which bears the image of perfect repose. Does not labour imply fatigue? Is it not a chastisement imposed upon man in consequence of a prevarication which caused him to fall from the prerogatives of his primitive state? And moreover, before that catastrophe had impaired the harmony of our faculties and drawn down the divine malediction upon earth, what would have been the object of labour to us, either of body or mind? These reflections so much the more prove to me the necessity of exactly defining the labour required of man in the design of his creation.

To labour is to act. We may act with pain; but pain is not a part of the essence of labour. Its essence is summed up in that energetic and glorious word: to act. Now, you do not suppose that God, who made all things, has destined man to eternal idleness. The most insignificant being, in coming into the world, brings into it a mission corresponding to the end for which it was created, a mission or a function which it accomplishes by labour. The very worm of the earth does something, it performs its task, it cooperates for an end; it belongs to the sacred band of useful creatures. How should man, raised so high by his faculties and by the place which he occupies in the universe, have received no other function than that of sterile idleness? It could not so be, and it was not the language of idle repose that God addressed to man, when at the hour of his birth he said to him: *Increase and multiply, and fill the earth, and subdue it, and rule over the fishes of the sea, and the fowls of the air, and all living creatures that move upon the earth.*[2] It was not a lesson of idleness that God gave him in bringing before him—according to the history of Genesis—*all the animals of creation, that he might give them a name which should explain their nature and remain to them for ever.*[3] In fine, when he led him to a dwelling-place, called by Scripture the Paradise of Pleasure, it was not to slumber there in the sleep of inaction; for it is said God placed him there *to dress it and to keep it*—UT OPERARETUR ET CUSTODIRET ILLUM.[4] Do not then unite in your minds the idea of perfection and happiness, or even the idea of repose, with that of inactivity or idleness. God was infinite activity before he assumed, in the creation and government of the world, a work worthy of all his attributes; by an eternal action he produced in himself the Word which ever speaks to him, the Holy Ghost which responds to both; by a fecundity as ancient as himself he diffused

[2] Genesis i. 28.   [3] Ibid. ii. 19.   [4] Ibid. ii. 15.

between three the unity of an essence whose inner movement is perfection, beatitude, and repose. So far from the idea of action—which is that of labour—being incompatible with the notion of a happy and perfect state, it is the necessary element which constitutes all that we know of that state; for, to think is to act, to will is to act, to love is to act, and apparently none of these acts will be rejected from the definition of happiness and perfection.

Placed in the centre of created things, belonging by his soul to the higher world of spirits, by his body to the lower world of nature, having the earth for passage and God for end, man was indebted by a double labour to a double function. His first function was to tend towards God who had given him truth that he might know him, charity that he might love him, the participation of his own life as perspective and term, but with all these gifts the gift also of liberty, which, raising him to the glory of a person master of himself, permitted him to repudiate his legitimate end, and opened before him the honourable but perilous career of virtue. This was the first work, the great work of man. However pure he might have been in his soul and body, he was free; he could withdraw from God and perish. Prayer, reflection, vigilance, perpetual care of his heart, were necessary for him to prevent his falling from the virginal splendour in which God created him.

Our present state includes other difficulties, which leave us no doubt as to the importance of the spiritual work imposed upon the human race. The abuse of liberty has covered every part of our being with ruins; our intelligence is darkened; our love has grown cold; the struggle between good and evil has assumed a character of alarming depth, with the development of generations. God, without disappearing from our midst, has found amongst us enemies conspiring against the remembrance of him, and employing all the resources of the mind and the passions to destroy that remembrance. There is no tradition which has not been denied, no duty which has not been outraged, no divine institution which has not been subjected to the violent attacks of mad impiety; and if God has remained visible during the whole course of ages, if he still reigns over the posterity of his first creature, it is but at the price of a combat rife in tears and blood. You are engaged in this divine war, you form part of it, and, victors or vanquished, I have nothing to teach you on the painful price of truth.

Even had we but the work of the soul; if man could extend towards God a look free from all other care, a hand free from all other burden! But it is not so.

From the first, a function and a labour of a different order have been confided to us. God, because he would not leave us without occupation for the forces of the body by which we hold to the inferior world, called us to share his temporal government. He gave us the earth to guard and fertilise, not at first at the price of our toil, but by an administration which partook of the nature of empire and added to our other prerogatives the glory of useful command. In exchange for a royal and blessed culture, the obedient earth rendered back to us a substance necessary to sustain our immortality during its earthly existence. *Behold*, said God to us, *I have given you every herb bearing seed upon the earth, and all trees that have in themselves seed of their own kind, to be your meat.*[5] This reciprocal intercourse between nature and man possessed nothing primitively which was an obstacle to the relation between our soul and God. The soul rather found therein a spiritual aliment, a source of joy which sprang forth without effort and reached even to its author. But that state did not last, and you know what temporal labour has become for the posterity of Adam. A curse has fallen upon it; the earth, which yielded to our desires, refuses to us all that we do not pay it for beforehand in toil and

[5] Genesis i. 29.

fatigue; it doles out its gifts to us with avarice that nothing can move, with uncertainty that nothing can disarm. Nearly the whole of the human race, with brow bent towards it, implores it with assiduous devotedness, and gathers for recompense only the bitter bread of hard poverty. Now poverty of the body easily entails that of the soul: it has created modes of servitude which draw all the human faculties together in their many folds, and, by pressing upon their action, plunges them into a state approaching to death. Man descends towards the instinct of the animal; absorbed in his material wants, he forgets his origin and his end; he throws to the winds the divine life whose germ is within him, and his only care is to force the earth to render to him the blessings of eternity.

We can only accuse ourselves; God is not responsible for our faults and our blindness. He foresaw them, doubtless; and I have told you why, notwithstanding that prevision, he did not refuse us the blessing of liberty. But, since he foresaw them, his wisdom and his goodness commanded him to come to our help, and, by a primitive, fundamental, and imprescriptible law, to regulate the relation between temporal and spiritual labour, both necessary to mankind, the one as the principle of its divine life, the other as the principle of its terrestrial life; both of which should be reciprocally limited in an equitable proportion. Now, who should have discovered this, and who should have established that proportion, if God had not done it? Who should have had wisdom to determine the time which man owed to his soul, and that which he owed to his body? Who should have possessed the authority necessary, in so difficult a matter, to obtain the sanction of universal respect? Who should have saved man from the tyranny of his own cupidity, and from the tyranny, not less to be feared, of one stronger than himself? In the question of labour lies the root of all servitude; it is the question of labour which has made masters and servants, conquering and conquered nations, oppressors of every kind and oppressed of every name. Labour being no other thing than human activity, everything necessarily has relation to it, and according as it is well or ill distributed, society is well or ill organized, happy or miserable, moral or immoral. We have now before us a proof of this which the most blind are obliged to comprehend. What has agitated the world during the last twenty years? What is the cry of the civil wars which we now witness? Is it not: *Organization of labour?* Is it not also: *Live by labour or die fighting?* And, if we examine the chain of historical revolutions, shall we ever find for them, whatever may be their name, another primary cause than the question of labour? The migrations of nations, the invasion of the barbarians, the servile wars, the troubles of the forum, all the great human agitations, hang directly or indirectly upon that terrible question, which rises again from its own ashes with obstinate immortality. It is the axis upon which the destinies of the world turn.

And, consequently, the first religious and civil law is the law of labour. Now who should, who could, lay it down? Who, save He who owes nothing to any one, but who, having from love made himself the father of minds, willed to be the light whence they should derive their direction? Who, save He who has created the soul and the body of man, who knows their wants, who has measured their powers, and who alone possesses the secret of limits, because he has none? It was just that, in the act of creation, God should promulgate all the bases of the physical, moral, and religious orders, and that he should promulgate them by acts sufficiently powerful for the remembrance of them to bear their commandment even to the last generations. Language alone would not have sufficed ; God was not content to proclaim his laws by language alone, at the origin of things any more than on Sinai and Calvary. He has constantly graven them in **acts** whose eloquence is more enduring than brass. The cross of Calvary, the tables of Sinai, the waves of the deluge, the days of creation, are the four great monuments of divine legislation; imperishable monuments, which, after so many ages, exist in all the vigour of the first day. The cross of Calvary covers the five divisions of the world; the tables of Sinai are read in all the places crowned by the cross; the waves of the deluge have left their traces from the Alps to the Caucasus, from the Caucasus to the Himalayas, from the Himalayas to the summit of the Andes: and the days of the creation, religiously preserved in the strata of the globe, in the furrows of our ploughs, revive that magnificent law of labour which has preceded all others, and which we must now more clearly define to you.

You have already heard the terms of this law; *God, it is said, ended on the seventh day the work which he had made, and he rested on the seventh day from all his work which he had done, and he blessed the seventh day and sanctified it, because in it he rested from all his work which God created and made.* Such is the proportion of temporal to spiritual labour, of the labour of the body to the labour of the soul, according as God determined it by the sovereign example of his own work. And, indeed, if the question had depended upon man, we may be sure that it would not have been solved in this manner. Knowing the law, are we even capable of explaining it to ourselves? Why should the number seven express the totality of the two kinds of labour? Why should spiritual labour amount only to a seventh part of temporal labour? Why should the one occupy six consecutive days, and not a longer or a shorter time? Is there nothing in the powers of the body and the soul that leads us to this proportion of six to one? Or is it nature that reveals it to us by the general harmony of its laws? No, gentlemen, neither do the phenomena of nature, nor the necessities of the body, nor the wants of the soul, give us the elements of such an induction. When the rationalist dictators of the French Revolution, from hatred of all traditional and sacred origins, resolved to efface the ancient period of seven days from the calendar of a great people, they knew not where to take the basis of a new calculation, save in the convenience of a system of numeration. They decreed that the week should be ten days, in order to introduce the uniformity of the decimal mode into labour, as into weights and measures. The French citizen was to labour for nine days and rest on the tenth, simply because a like division had been established in things of number, and because it is easier to compute figures by this mode than by any other. No one troubled himself to learn whether the body of man would bear such an increase of labour ; and, had they done this, it is manifest that every precise limit would have been the result of an arbitrary choice, and not the fruit of experience or reasoning.

The number seven, chosen by God, has no relation to any mathematical fitness. Nor is it justified by the degree of the bodily forces ; for it is not easy to see, for instance, that man would not have been able to labour for seven days and to rest on the eighth. It is a number taken from a higher region than physical order, and so it should be, since it was a matter of regulating the relations of two kinds of labour, one material and the other spiritual. Evidently, between two kinds of things so completely diverse, the mediator could come only from a point which governed both, that is to say, the soul and the body. Now, God alone governs all the beings which compose the hierarchy of the universe ; he alone, in his universal and creating essence, possesses the pattern of their own, the reason of their existence, the law of their relations, the principle of their harmony. It is then in himself, in the higher and mysterious mathematics of his own nature, that God has chosen the number suitable as the rule of our double activity. This number does not appear in the work of cosmogony only, it plays an important part in all the rest of the divine operations, as the Scriptures show us. We see it shining in the seven weeks of years of the Hebrew jubilee, in the seven branches of the candlestick of Jerusalem, in the seven gifts of the Holy Ghost, in the seven sacraments of the Church, in the seven seals of the Apocalypse, and in a multitude of occurrences which it would require too much time to enumerate. In almost every page of the sacred books its importance is manifested, by the use which God has directly or indirectly made of it.

In short, to the eyes of pure reason the number seven is an arbitrary number; to the eyes of reason enlightened by faith it is a divine number; to the eyes of history it is a traditional number; to the eyes of experience it is a number which has reconciled the wants and duties of the body with the wants and duties of the soul. Six days of temporal labour have sufficed for man in all times and under all climates to gain his subsistence without weakening his strength, to fertilise the earth without compromising his health or his happiness; the seventh day, consecrated to repose in the worship of God, has also sufficed for him to refresh his soul, to preserve truth, to rekindle his love, and, in fine, to advance peacefully and joyously towards the august end of a creature blessed by God. Whatever metaphysical judgment you may pronounce upon this memorable division of temporal and spiritual labour, there are two things which you cannot deny, namely: its universality and its efficacity; so much the more remarkable, as we do not see any rational cause for it, whilst we are forced to conclude that that cause exists. Would you destroy the balance of human activity, engender the degradation of souls, the oppression of the weak, the cupidity of all, and the misery of the greater number? Would you do this? It is easy; touch the law of labour as it was promulgated by the work of creation; increase temporal labour; lessen, by violence or artifice, spiritual labour; abandon man to the inspirations of his covetousness and the will of his masters; do this, and you will be sure to gather its fruit in a generation which will satisfy you, if you like the moral and physical degradation of mankind.

I say the physical as well as the moral degradation; for the observance of the seventh day was not established simply with a view to religious sanctification, but also and directly with a view to terrestrial preservation. This is why Scripture employs two remarkable expressions at the same time; it says that God *rested* on the seventh day, and that he *sanctified* it. And as the object of God was to trace the rule of our activity by his example, it follows that he recommended two things to us at the same time, repose and the sanctification of the seventh day. And if you doubt this, if you do not think that God has so great a regard for the equitable well-being of the body of man, hear it again proclaimed by Moses, at the foot of Sinai, in the great law of the Sabbath : *Six days shalt thou labour, and shalt do all thy works; the seventh day is the day of the sabbath, that is, the rest of the Lord thy God; thou shalt not do any work therein, thou nor thy son nor thy daughter, nor thy man-servant nor thy maid-servant, nor thy ox, nor thy ass, nor any of thy beasts, nor the stranger that is within thy gates.*[6] This is the law. Now listen to the reason which God immediately gives for it; *that*, he says, *thy man-servant and thy maid-servant may rest even as thyself.*[7] And going still further, he said on another occasion to all the assembled people : *Six days thou shalt work; the seventh day thou shalt cease, that thy ox and thy ass may rest, and the son of thine handmaid and the stranger may be refreshed.*[8] Here God stipulates in favour of the animals who share the labour of man; he associates them in the benefit of his merciful providence, and

[6] Deuteronomy v. 13, 14.   [7] Ibid.
[8] Exodus xxiii. 12.

The Double Work of Man. 249

since they are fatigued with the reasonable creature, he wills that the repose of the reasonable creature should extend even to them. You recognise here the heart of God, and if your intelligence still doubted of the temporally philanthropic sense attached by Scripture to the law of the seventh day, there remains no longer any excuse for you before texts which from their clearness defy interpretation. Listen again, however. After God had recommended to his people the observance of the seventh day in favour of the poorest and most laborious, he terminates by this solemn adjuration: *Remember that thou also didst serve in Egypt, and the Lord thy God brought thee out from thence with a strong hand and a stretched-out arm: Therefore he hath commanded thee that thou shouldst observe the sabbath day.*[9] Thus it is in remembrance of the bondage in Egypt, and in recalling it to them, that God imposes upon the posterity of Jacob the charter of rest from labour, that is to say, the first and fundamental charter of all liberty. For what is the liberty of a man attached to the glebe of unremitting labour? What is the liberty of a body never uplifted towards the vault of heaven, and the liberty of a soul never raised towards the light of God?

It is to you, gentlemen, to all generations of

[9] Deuteronomy v. 15.

masters, that these formidable words are addressed, which, three thousand years ago, resounded in the deserts of the Red Sea: Remember that thou also didst serve in Egypt! All of us, in our forefathers, have served; all of us, in our posterity, shall serve in Egypt. In vain do we wear the signs of emancipation, and ask from the future the fidelity which it refuses to kings; we are of a blood which servile labour has formed, which servile labour will form again. See in your hands the trace of earth; we come from the earth, and to it we shall return. There is no exception for any one of us, for the child of the palace any more than for the child of the cottage. Sooner or later the long hand of misfortune will again seize upon us and bring us back to the obscure labour which was our cradle. And if it was so in the ages of stability, how much more now when every corner-stone has been destroyed, and we build in the tempests of equality the shifting edifice of our destinies. Harken then to the words which remind you of the bondage of Egypt, respect in your brethren living in service the service which was your own, and which will return to you again. Take not away from them the day of relaxation which was prepared for them from the beginning as the liberty of their souls and bodies, and with a degree of munificence of which you do not perhaps form an idea.

For remark that God has not made of the seventh day a private institution, a day to take at hazard by each of us in any particular course of occupied days. No, he has made of it the great social institution; he has convoked the human race on the same day and at the same hour in the whole course of ages, inviting it to repose, to rejoice, and be exalted in him. In a word, he has founded a periodical and perpetual festival for mankind. For man needs festivals. Withheld far from the permanent city which is the term of his pilgrimage, and bearing in his heart the sadness of this trial of absence, he needs, by certain emotions, to leave the monotonous shadow of his life. Like Saul, he needs to hear the sound of the harp, or like David, to dance to music before the ark of God. But who will give these festivals to the poor of this world? Who will give them palaces, statues, paintings, voices, and lights? Who will give them emotions worthy of them, and that rare joy in which the conscience is enraptured as well as the heart? The people are poor and without art; they possess nothing great but themselves and God who protects them. The people and God come together and form the festival of mankind. For sixty centuries these two have been faithful to this meeting, and enjoy together without interruptions that festival which costs nothing to the people but their assembling, to God but looking down upon them.

The legislators of nations have recognised this popular want of common and public enjoyments; they have sought to satisfy it by religious pomps, by spectacles, triumphs, games, and combats. But instead of instructing and elevating man, nothing has helped more to degrade him; the most shameful passions came there to seek gratification and applause. Sensuality and blood met together there before the sacred images of country; and publicity, the mother of modesty, is there for the multitude only an additional debauch. This is because, in fact, the pleasures of the crowd turn easily towards all the vices. A celebrated politician has said: "Whoever assembles the people makes them factious." It may with no less truth be said: Whoever amuses the people corrupts them. In modern times rationalist legislators have been seen endeavouring to create festivals in order to replace that of the seventh day which they had abolished. They have only succeeded in inventing imitations of antiquity with the addition of ridicule and without the people. Public common sense was too just and too profound, under the inspiration of

Christianity, to enjoy these puerile renovations. It then became necessary, in the great occasions of civil life, to limit them to vulgar amusements, and God alone remained to give to the human race grave solemnities which draw men together, move, ameliorate, and bring them repose.

Is there any one among you who has not been touched by the spectacle which a Christian population presents on the day consecrated to God? The public places covered with a multitude of beings dressed in their best apparel; all ages appearing there with their hopes and fears, each tempered by a sentiment higher than life. The eyes that meet each other are animated by fraternal joy; the servant is nearer to his master; the poor less removed from the rich; all, by the community of the same duty accomplished and the same grace received, feel more fully that they are sons of the same Father who is in heaven. The silence of servile labour is compensated for by the joyous and musical sound of the bells, which make known to thousands of men that they are free, and prepares them to endure for God the days when they will not be free. No austerity clouds their features; the idea of observance is moderated by that of repose, and the idea of repose is embellished by the image of a festival. Incense burns in the temple; lights shine upon the altars; music fills the vaults and speaks to all hearts; the priest goes from the people to God and from God to the people; earth mounts upwards and heaven descends. Who does not leave the temple more calm? Who will not return to it better? Oh! for my part, gentlemen, this day has never passed without having moved me; and even here, in this capital, where so many souls do not respect it, I never witness its popular effect without lifting my heart towards God in an aspiration of gratitude and love.

Such is then the sense, such is the result of that great law of labour which God willed to promulgate and to hallow in the very act of creation. After having interpreted it to you, can I withhold a painful sensation which oppresses me? Can I refrain from complaining that there is a Christian people which despises this law, and that people is our own? Is it really France that, in this point, neglects the most sacred of duties between man and man? Is it France that tears in twain the fundamental pact of mankind, that delivers over to the rich the body and soul of the poor to use at their pleasure, that tramples under foot the day of liberty, equality, fraternity, the sublime day of the people and of God? I ask you, is it really France? Do not excuse her by saying that she grants to each the free exercise of his own worship, and that no one, against his consent, is constrained to work on the seventh day. For it is but to add to the reality of servitude the hypocrisy of freedom. Ask the workman whether he is free to abandon his labour on the dawn of the day that commands him to rest. Ask the young man who consumes his life in a daily lucre of which he does not profit, if he is free to breathe only once in the week the air of heaven and the still purer air of truth. Ask those withered creatures who people the manufacturing cities if they are free to save their souls in comforting their bodies. Ask the innumerable victims of personal cupidity and of the cupidity of a master, if they are free to become better, and if the gulf of toil without physical or moral reparation does not swallow them up alive. Ask those even who repose, but who repose in the degradation of unregulated passions, ask them what becomes of the people in that rest which is not given and protected by God. No, gentlemen, liberty of conscience here is only a veil that covers oppression; it covers with a golden mantle the cowardly shoulders of the most vile of all tyranny, the tyranny that abuses the toil of man by cupidity and impiety. If liberty of conscience were a reality here, doubtless Protestant England would have perceived it; doubtless the democracy of the United States of America would have learned it : and where in the world has the right of the seventh day been more respected? Learn, then, those who know it not; learn, enemies of God and of the human race, whatever name they bear, that between the strong and the weak, between the rich and the poor, between the master and the servant, it is liberty that oppresses, and law that gives freedom. Right is the sword of the powerful, duty is the shield of the weak.

It is high time for us to remove from France this lamentable error, which has lasted but too long. The tempests also warn us that it is not good to violate commandments which were promulgated with the creation, renewed in the thunders of Sinai, and reinvigorated by the blood of Calvary. Whosoever is against God is against mankind, and if a few unhappy men, armed with what they call reason, fear not to make these two enemies, we may trust to the vengeance of the future alone—that future which is already the present, and which warns us all to think of our faults and generously to combat them by a salutary reparation. France will do this! Yes, Lord, France will do this! We see its foreshadowing in the respect she pays to thee in the midst of the ruins she has so suddenly made. She will listen to

The Double Work of Man.

the forewarnings of experience, she will rise again towards thee by the difficulties which surround her, she will recognise the principle of her salvation in that beautiful saying which thou hast pronounced to all nations of the earth by Jesus Christ thine only Son : *Seek first the Kingdom of God, and his justice, and all other things shall be added to you.*[10] Hearken, O God, to that voice which speaks to thee from France; and when another year fallen from thy eternity upon our short life shall bring us again together in this temple, grant that we may find here more steadfast, stronger, and more glorious than ever, our country and truth !

[10] Matt. vi. 33.

DECLARATION.

ALTHOUGH I have constantly taught under the authority and in the presence of the archbishops of Paris, and my doctrine has never been criticised or called in question by them; although that same doctrine, published by the press, has excited neither reproach nor discussion: yet, lest in treating so many theological questions some involuntary error may have escaped me, and this I must and do readily presume from my weakness, I declare that I submit my Conferences to the Catholic Church, whose son I am, and in particular to the Holy Roman Church, the mother and mistress of all Churches, wherein resides the plenitude of the authority founded upon earth by our Lord Jesus Christ.

I also declare again that I do not acknowledge the pretended reproductions of my Conferences which

www.ingramcontent.com/pod-product-compliance
Lightning Source LLC
Chambersburg PA
CBHW031624160426
43196CB00006B/273